Where Was God When I Cried?

D0111451

Where Was God When I Cried?

Kay Twombley

Treasure House

An Imprint of
Destiny Image₀ **Publishers, Inc.**
P.O. Box 310
Shippensburg, PA 17257-0310

"For where your treasure is,
there will your heart be also." Matthew 6:21

ISBN 1-56043-304-3

For Worldwide Distribution
Printed in the U.S.A.

First Printing: 1998   Second Printing: 1998

This book and all other Destiny Image, Revival Press,
and Treasure House books are available
at Christian bookstores and distributors worldwide.

For a U.S. bookstore nearest you, call **1-800-722-6774**.
For more information on foreign distributors, call **717-532-3040**.
Or reach us on the Internet: **http://www.reapernet.com**

Dedication

This book is dedicated to all the women and men who have been used and abused physically, sexually, emotionally, and/or verbally.

You may feel that no one cares. You may have told a family member or friend about the abuse, only to be treated as if it were your fault. Some of you have never told anyone, thinking that somehow you should have been able to handle it yourself.

You may have had a taste of God at an early age. However, this taste did not last long because of the intrusion of pain and betrayal into your life. God wants to build on that taste with you today as you begin to read this book. Your appetite for God has not vanished, or you would not even have this book in your hand.

The Holy Spirit is with you today to increase your appetite and unravel your pain and betrayal so you can be set free to love as you have always wanted to love. Be encouraged as you begin reading this book. God has protected your spirit. It is alive and waiting to be fed by His Holy Spirit.

Dedication

This book is dedicated to all the women and men who have been used and abused physically, sexually, emotionally, and/or verbally.

You may feel that no one cares. You may have told a family member or friend about the abuse, only to be treated as if it were your fault. Some of you have never told anyone, thinking that somehow you should have been able to handle it yourself.

You may have had a taste of God at an early age. However, this taste did not last long because of the intrusion of pain and betrayal into your life. God wants to build on that taste with you today as you begin to read this book. Your appetite for God has not vanished, or you would not even have this book in your hand.

The Holy Spirit is with you today to increase your appetite and unravel your pain and betrayal so you can be set free to love as you have always wanted to love. Be encouraged as you begin reading this book. God has protected your spirit. It is alive and waiting to be fed by His Holy Spirit.

Acknowledgments

I would like to thank several people whose skill, love, and support helped me write and publish this book. First, though, I thank my Father God, who gave me the idea for this book. He, Father God, cares so much for the wounded that He has provided this book to help bring more healing to the hurting. Thank You, Father, for allowing me to be one of Your vessels of Your healing power.

I thank Sandra Miller, my dear friend. Because of her love for the Lord, she spent many hours on the original manuscript proofing for misspelled words, rearranging sentences, and correcting grammar. I also appreciate being constantly held up in prayer by the R&R Ministries prayer warriors: Jackie, Madge, Greg, Dick, Carolyn, Richard, Lisa, Ruby, Mary, Martha, Virginia, Terri, Linda, Ruth, and Cheryl. Thank you for your steadfastness.

My husband, Mike, has always been there for me with a wise and encouraging word. His comments have been invaluable. Mike has been so willing to sacrifice his convenience to help me do what I needed to do to complete the book. Thank you, Mike, for believing in this work. I thank my children, Kathy and Ashley, too for being so supportive throughout the entire writing of this manuscript.

Thank you to the team at Treasure House: Libby, Staff Publisher; Julie, Staff Editor; Tony, Graphic Artist for the cover; and Phillip, Acquisition Editor. Each of you demonstrated dedication to the Father's heart on each phase of this work. May God bless each of you mightily as you continue to bring the love of God to the people.

The anointed line drawings in this book are the creation of Cliff Hawley, of San Antonio, Texas. Thank you to you, Cliff, and to your wife for your dedication to this work of the Father's.

I thank, love, and appreciate my mother, Elizabeth Weatherford. Without her love and guidance, I would not be where I am today. She taught me to pray and to believe that God can handle anything. Each day of her life she has demonstrated steadfastness. She has never wavered from the Lord. She prayed for me, my sister Lois, and my brothers Mike and Tad, and we are all serving the Lord. She prayed fervently for 25 years for my dad's salvation; he accepted the Lord when he was 45. My dad lived until he was 76. My dad, Marion Weatherford, taught me that Christ can turn a person's heart completely around as He did his. My dad's life was a demonstration of the power of God. Thank you, Dad, for allowing the Father God to do such a powerful work in your life.

May God abundantly bless each of you who have helped on this manuscript.

Contents

Introduction

As a counselor I have often been faced with difficult questions. One of the most difficult and troubling questions that people have asked is this: Where was God when a child was being sexually, physically, and/or emotionally abused? I remember being faced with that in my office one day and not knowing what to say. That night I went home and cried out to God for some answers. How was I supposed to tell people that God is a loving, kind, caring God who wants to heal their every wound when they couldn't understand, nor could I explain, where He was when they suffered some type of horrible abuse?

I began my personal journey to answer the question, "Where was God when I cried?" by praying and asking God how to help people who have been bruised and battered emotionally. However, as I was searching for an answer to give to the people I counseled, I realized it was an answer that I needed for myself.

I had never questioned God before. I grew up knowing that there was a God and I believed that He was good. Yet, after listening in therapy sessions to heartrending stories of abuse, I started questioning why an all-loving, all-powerful God allowed these things to happen.

This book was birthed from my own need to answer that question. During my search for answers, the Father showed me many things, which I will share with you in the following chapters. Among the topics I will discuss are these: how abuse affects the abused person, how one can receive healing from abuse, how to move forward spiritually when one really has no desire to move forward, and where God was during the abuse.

Basically, this is a book about sifting, sorting, and unraveling. Sometimes we need help in doing that. My hope is that this book will help you grapple with the issues in your past that may be haunting you, holding you back, and keeping you locked in a mind-set of loneliness, bitterness, hopelessness, and despair. My prayer is that this book will aid you in untangling yourself, so that you can move on and experience the freedom that is possible through God.

You may be doubtful about the possibility of ever being healed from events in your past. But be encouraged—there *is* a God and He does care! It may take a while for you to get the answers and the healing that you need, but be persistent. You may even have to read this book several times to digest the information and guidance. Pray before you continue. If you cannot pray, just say to God right now, *"God, please help me."*

Chapter 1

Looking for the Answer

For we have not an high priest which cannot be touched with the feeling of our infirmities; but was in all points tempted like as we are, yet without sin. Let us therefore come boldly unto the throne of grace, that we may obtain mercy, and find grace to help in time of need (Hebrews 4:15-16).

This book started with the intent of answering the title question, "Where was God?" However, I realized that many times people are too emotionally wounded to come to any satisfying answer by themselves. In order to help someone resolve this question, I felt that he must first experience some level of healing. Therefore this book begins with working through the healing process.

Most people have difficulty expressing what they feel—assuming that they know what they are feeling. Most do not realize what is blocking their feelings. I want this book to help you honestly and openly express your doubt and confusion.

You may face many obstacles as you attempt to resolve the question that the title of this book has posed. Your biggest problem may be your desire to find the answer quickly. You could say that is the track of least resistance.

Many beginning to read this book may be so exhausted with life that they are not sure they have the energy to wrestle with this issue. Motivation and enthusiasm for the things of God may be gone. Many of you need encouragement. You need to be told you can make it.

There is woundedness everywhere. On Sunday morning in church, every day in the schools, each night in the night clubs, and every moment in the prisons you find wounded people. "War stories" of abuse can be swapped at almost any gathering.

I believe the need for the Lord Jesus Christ is greater than ever. The Scripture says in Luke 4:18 that Jesus came to heal the brokenhearted:

The Spirit of the Lord is upon Me, because He hath anointed Me to preach the gospel to the poor; He hath sent Me to heal the brokenhearted, to preach deliverance to the captives, and recovering of sight to the blind, to set at liberty them that are bruised.

Many are bruised emotionally and are trying desperately to hang on to their belief in God. They want to have a fruitful Christian life, but they do not have any idea how to resolve the invisible barriers separating them from God.

Many reading this book have suffered disasters. Disasters come in all forms of emotional disappointments. Disasters have a tendency to haunt us. You may have suffered a disaster that is not your fault. You have suffered innocently and silently. You may have realized very young that life is unfair. You may feel like a victim.

I believe that God is drawing His people to Him for healing. I believe that many people who read this book want to move toward God, but have issues in them that are alive and they do not know what to do about those issues. I believe that many reading will prioritize their lives and take concrete steps that will help them please the Father.

I invite you to confront your feelings and try to find the truth about your life. The truth is generally never easy to face. However, the Bible says that the truth will set you free (see Jn. 8:32). Because truth hurts, we often protect ourselves from it. If we refuse to look at the truth, we put ourselves in a position of missing God. I want you to bring all your strong feelings straight to God as you read this book. God accepts and understands you just as you are. He is ready to heal your broken and hurting parts.

I invite you to consider allowing God to move in your life in a miraculous way as you read through these pages. You may say, "Oh yes, I believe in miracles." Actually, I think people want to believe, but believing is really harder than most admit. Many have unspoken doubts. The opposite of doubt is when people say that we see miracles every day. In one sense we do; a baby being conceived and born, or a cut healing on its own, are

miracles. But you have to remember that these occur-
rences happen to non-believers just as frequently as to
believers. Jesus said that He came so we would have life
and have it more abundantly (see Jn. 10:10b). The dictionary says that a miracle is something that happens
beyond human or natural powers. Most of us feel it is
quite natural for most cuts to heal unless the person's
natural defenses are somehow impaired. When Jesus
healed the blind and the lame, that was not natural;
that was supernatural. God is a supernatural God who
wants to reveal Himself to you.

I want to stretch your mind by the words on these
pages. I want you to have a greater understanding of
God. I want you to be expectant. I want you to see that
the way you are handling life now is probably a direct
result of how you were treated as a child. Your opinion
of God has been influenced by those life experiences. I
want you to be ready to allow the Father to move in
your life as we go through these pages. You may feel
you are like the man in John 5:5-9:

> *And a certain man was there, which had an infirmity*
> *thirty and eight years. When Jesus saw him lie, and*
> *knew that he had been now a long time in that case,*
> *He saith unto him, Wilt thou be made whole? The im-*
> *potent man answered Him, Sir, I have no man, when*
> *the water is troubled, to put me in the pool: but while*
> *I am coming, another steppeth down before me. Jesus*
> *saith unto him, Rise, take up thy bed, and walk. And*
> *immediately the man was made whole, and took up*
> *his bed, and walked....*

This man was so crippled, he couldn't go any farther. He had come to the closest place he could get to, to be near the place of help. God met him there. I believe God will meet you here in this book. Some of us need someone to help us move closer. You have come as far as you can go on your own. God is not through with you yet. The best is yet to come for those who will hang on and persevere.

He heals the broken hearted, and binds up their wounds.

PSALM 147:3

Chapter 2

Holes in Our Souls

Realizing the Effects of Past Pain

He heals the brokenhearted and binds up their wounds (Psalm 147:3 NIV).

Few people realize how much the events of our past affect—and sometimes even control—our present lives. Many of us are unable to walk a healthy Christian life because we are still hurting from wounds we received in our past. Not every negative childhood event causes emotional wounds; however, some do. Most of us do not recognize what constitutes an emotional wound. If we do, we are not sure what to do about it. Until we seek and obtain understanding and healing for our wounds, we will still have difficulty bearing the spiritual fruit we desire.

A Personal Revelation

God illustrated this truth to me through a revelation He gave me several years ago. I was attending a Christian

Believer United ladies' conference in Ridgecrest, North Carolina. While the moderator was announcing the next speaker, she began to minister. She shared with the group that she believed that this day God was going to heal women who had been abused.

As she was speaking, I silently thanked God for leaders in the Body of Christ who acknowledge that there are many people in the Church who are hurting emotionally. As I sat there and listened to the lady, the Lord told me to pick up my pen and write. I did not hear an audible voice; it was just a deep "knowing" that the Father was going to tell me something.

I quietly shut my eyes so I could be completely with the Lord. I began seeing the outline of a body, which looked like it had been x-rayed. The next thing I saw was the x-rayed body scattered with holes. Silently I asked the Lord, "What is that?"

"That is you," He replied.

"What do You mean?" I asked.

He said, "That is a picture of your soul. Those are wounds from your childhood." I told the Lord that I did not understand because I had not been abused in the way the moderator was referring to abuse. The Lord said, "You have suffered emotionally in ways you are not even aware of. You have been going to conferences and to church all your life and you have listened attentively; but when you leave those meetings, all the Word that you gained slowly seeps out through those holes. Until those wounds are healed, you will not be a strong Christian."

For the first time I started getting a glimpse of why I had heard God's Word for years but had never been able to plant it deeply in my heart. I had faithfully gone to church, but as I well knew, it is possible to go to church every Sunday and still live in fear every day of the week. A person can go to church every Sunday and have absolutely no faith and not know God's Word.

The Lord told me that because of these holes, I was filled with doubt. I had doubt that God would be there for me when I needed Him. Could I really trust the heavenly Father? He said that I was wounded from all the years my earthly father drank, and that I needed healing for those wounds.

When a person is consumed with poor self-esteem and feelings of shame and embarrassment, it is hard to grow spiritually. Guarding and protecting emotional wounds takes time and energy. The Lord showed me that I needed healing deep in my being and that once the healing took place, I would be less preoccupied with my own sense of inferiority.

He said, "When you are healed of these wounds, you will be able to retain My Word." He told me that I would be able to stand up to the devil as never before.

Then I saw the x-rayed body again and this time the holes were filled with a material like plaster of paris. I remember saying to the Lord, "Lord, please don't use plaster of paris to fill my holes because when it gets wet it will leak." Then God said, "When I heal you, it will last."

God did something permanent inside me that day. He sealed up areas in which satan had been attacking me. It is hard to explain the effects of that day. The Lord healed areas in me that I didn't know were wounded. I realized later that those wounded areas had not been opened to the Lord. When I experienced some level of healing, these areas of my heart could now be claimed for the Lord.

As you read this, if you have a similar condition, I hope that you will ask the Father by His Holy Spirit to start filling your holes with His healing power. But don't rush this process. God speaks in many ways and through many people. He may give you an instant "knowing" as He did me, or He may give you some other understanding through Scriptures, a dream, or a sermon you hear. As you read this book, you could gain insight that you have needed for many years. Do not limit God in the way He may bring healing and understanding to you. Part of your healing could be instantaneous; part of it may be a process.

What Are These Holes and How Do We Get Them?

Generally speaking, holes are entry points of pain. The pain may be from neglect, abandonment, rejection, mistreatment, or abuse in any form. All these assault a person's soul, and all cause wounds that must be healed. Sometimes we don't remember or aren't aware of being hurt, but a hole punctures our soul regardless and usually manifests itself in some noticeable way later on.

As an example, let's look at how a fingernail develops. First the nail begins to grow behind the cuticle. This growth is invisible to the human eye. Then, as time goes by, this area grows out to where it is visible. If you do something that injures the fingernail while it is in the early growth stage, it causes a defect that becomes visible when the nail matures. You may not be aware of when or how the injury occurred, but you become aware that there was an injury because you can see its effect. This is a physical example of the way we develop emotionally—only emotional injuries cannot be clipped off as easily as an injured nail can be. Emotional injuries have to be resolved and healed.

When a human baby is born, he needs food, shelter, and clothing, and he needs to be loved and nurtured. A baby who does not get any nurturing will develop a syndrome called "failure to thrive," which can be fatal. The reason is simple: Human beings need love, nurturing, acceptance, and affirmation. Humans need to connect with other humans. Babies primarily need to connect with their parents. When that connection is not made or is interrupted, emotional injury occurs.

The opposite of love, acceptance, and affirmation is indifference, rejection, and discrediting (being overlooked). Whenever you experience rejection or whenever you are devalued or emotionally deprived in any way, you experience emotional injury to your soul.

When you were growing up, you could have encountered a multitude of circumstances that hurt you emotionally. Perhaps you lost a parent in a divorce or to death. If either parent was too busy for you, then you probably experienced emotional abandonment. If you lost a parent to death, then you experienced emotional and physical abandonment. If you were physically, sexually, or verbally abused by a parent or a significant other, then your soul was injured. If you were reared by an overprotective parent, you probably sustained wounds. In this case, parents who are too controlling send the message to a child that he is not smart enough or good enough to make decisions by himself, so the parent makes the decisions for him.

When a person is misused, abused, ignored, rejected, or abandoned, there is always emotional pain. It hurts when you are not valued. This pain causes the holes in our soul. This applies not only to childhood rejections, but also to present-day rejection. For instance, you may have had your emotional needs met as a child, but now you are suffering rejection from your mate. This rejection needs to be healed.

If You Have a Hole, You Suffered a Loss

For every hole there is a loss. This is a hard connection for some people to make. For example, if you were reared by an alcoholic parent, you lost a normal childhood. Your parent probably did not nurture you as you needed to be nurtured because he or she was too preoccupied with the addiction. If you were reared by an overcontrolling parent, you lost a healthy relationship with that parent. If you were sexually abused, you lost a normal relationship with the abuser, and more than that, you learned to distrust those in authority.

When you have holes in your soul that you haven't dealt with, you will most likely seek out other ways to make yourself feel better. These substitute "comforts" are often unhealthy responses that cause more harm to an already injured soul. (Unhealthy responses to pain are discussed in more detail in a later chapter.) Present-day stress will intensify this problem. When you stack present-day stress on top of unmet childhood needs, you have double trouble.

You may not even know that you have emotional injury, and if it becomes evident, you may not know what to do about it. We all need comfort, but many times we do not know how to tap into or access the Father's peace. You may have tried and tried to walk in holiness and feel like you have been a failure over and over. In reality you have never dealt with the main problem.

Dealing With the Heart of the Problem

Dealing with the heart of the problem involves several things. First, you have to identify and express the unmet needs and the hidden hurts in your life. Second, you have to recognize the losses you have suffered, and then allow yourself to grieve for what you lost.

I know that people, especially men, do not like to deal with terms of vulnerability, such as *loss* and *grieving,* and *even holes in your soul,* because dealing with these necessitates that we face up to our own weaknesses. I hope, dear reader, that if you're a man, you will not stop reading this book. Please stay with me as I explain this.

Men want to be strong, and rightly so. God gave men a seemingly instinctual desire to conquer. Generally, men have been the warriors and hunters in our society. This desire to be strong is the reason most men do not feel comfortable talking about their weaknesses. That is okay. However, if your past is controlling some part of your present (and this applies to both men and women), then you need to deal with it.

Ignoring or denying the holes in your soul will only leave you feeling helpless and frustrated, because it's like trying to carry water in a sieve. Your soul will not be able to hold on to all the truth that God wants to fill you with as long as you allow those holes to remain. With God's help you can yield to Him for healing, but you must have strength to deal with the heart of the problem. You may not be aware that you need healing or understanding. Ask God to give you understanding of your actual state. Believe God is with you to bring you revelation, healing, and understanding as you read this book.

*   *   *

Holy Father, let Your Holy Spirit rest on us as we seek You for understanding and healing. Many who have experienced losses in their lives may not be sure of how much You love them. Father, reveal to them how the losses have affected their attitude toward You. Father, let Your healing power flow over them as they continue to seek You for understanding and comfort. In Jesus' name. Amen.

I have seen your misery...
I have heard you cry out...
I am concerned about your suffering...
For I know your sorrows.

©1998

Trust me.

Chapter 3

Silence Associated With Emotional Pain

If an enemy were insulting me, I could endure it; if a foe were raising himself against me, I could hide from him. But it is you, a man like myself, my companion, my close friend, with whom I once enjoyed sweet fellowship as we walked with the throng at the house of God (Psalm 55:12-14 NIV).

According to Webster's Dictionary, *abuse* is "a deceitful act; deception; a corrupt practice or custom; improper use or treatment; physical maltreatment." In other words, any situation in which you have been lied to, mistreated, taken for granted, or overlooked is a form of abuse. When you are devalued in any situation, there is hurt and pain. If a husband, boyfriend, family member, or significant other has hurt you, there is emotional trauma. You may feel used and then discarded. In order to bring about healing in your life, those feelings need to be verbalized. You need to be able to say, "The person I loved most, the person I *trusted*, hurt me." Yet, for various reasons many people hold their pain inside. Thus they suffer in silence— fearful, confused, hurting, alone—unknowingly preventing themselves from obtaining the very healing that they long for.

Silence seems to be associated with emotional pain. Whether the mistreatment is in the form of neglect in the home of an alcoholic, or emotional abandonment in the home of an excessively busy parent, or domination in the home of the parent who exercises overcontrol, or betrayal and violation in the home of a child being sexually abused, it all affects the victim. All these forms of mistreatment deny the child one thing: parental approval.

We all need parental approval. When that approval is missing, silence replaces the ability to express emotions. The alcoholic could not give approval because he was too involved in his addiction. The preoccupied parent could not give approval because he was gone all the time. The overcontrolling parent could not offer approval because he was too busy correcting the child. Because of the severity of sexual abuse, a violated child has no respect for his parents' approval.

Another reason silence is such a part of a painful past is a suffering person's inability to untangle their feelings. When you should have received love and affection from your parents and you did not, there is a sense of confusion. You develop a "love-hate" relationship. You love your parents because they are your parents, but you have this other negative emotion that is very much alive.

Lonely Silence

There is a specific silence associated with sexual abuse. Perhaps you're saying, "But I've been silent for so long. I don't even know how to begin." You may not understand the reason for your silence. Maybe you think that you'd hurt too many people if you told what happened. Maybe you're afraid that no one will believe you. These feelings are especially common when the person who abused you is a family member or is a close friend of the family.

Maybe you've kept silent because the person who abused you warned you that if you told anyone, terrible things would happen to you and your family members. Maybe the abuser tried to convince you that your interpretation of what happened is wrong. He tried to convince you that the abuse did not occur or that you did something to deserve it. The violator wants to control your mind by convincing you that his sin is not there.

What a horrible trick to play! Someone hurts you and then says it did not happen! What a feeling of entrapment! You know the truth. Anger swells within you with no way to be vented. You feel you must bear the burden alone. You somehow push this information as far down mentally as you are able so you can try to make some sense out of everything. (This can also apply to other forms of abuse or mistreatment.)

Over the years I have heard many stories of an abuser trying to convince the victim that the abusive event either did not happen or that it did not happen the way the victim perceived it. The person who tries to convince the victim that the event did not happen generally has a very strong personality, and the victim usually does not know how to handle the deception. When I hear abuse victims describe this scenario, I sense such a feeling of helplessness. Not only does the person have to suffer the abuse or mistreatment, but now he must defend the truth while the violator tries to vindicate himself by claiming it did not happen. To stand up to this deluded way of thinking takes real strength, and many times the victim of the mistreatment gives up fighting because standing up for the truth is too hard.

What Happens When You Feel Like No One Cares?

There is a unique loneliness that sets in when you are unable to share with anyone that you have been betrayed. The pain is even greater if you did share what happened and the person refused to believe what you said. You may have cried out to God, but even He didn't seem to care—after all, He allowed the abuse to happen in the first place.

Since the people in your life who should have loved you the most violated or betrayed you, you struggle to understand what real love is all about. You feel very fearful and alone. The loneliness that sets in when you feel no one cares about you is a feeling that reaches deep into your being and helps you build invisible barriers. You want to limit the contact you have with people because people have hurt you, so you build walls to protect yourself from further abuse. You now have become emotionally fortified or walled in. You have sealed yourself off from the people who hurt you and, without realizing it, you have sealed yourself off from God.

No Matter What It Feels Like, You're Not Alone

When you are living behind defensive walls, you are oppressed. You are a prisoner of your own thoughts. Jesus came to set the captives free. He wants you to be free to love and be loved. The hurdle you must get over is not a tangible hurdle. It is a mental and spiritual one. You must realize that the enemy, the devil, wants you to keep your old mind-set—the mind-set that says, "I can handle everything on my own without anyone's help." We have Scripture after Scripture promising that God will be there if we seek after Him.

God Hears Your Cry

As I was looking for clues to help me understand this issue, I came across a very interesting Scripture in Exodus 3:7 (NIV):

> *The Lord said, "I have indeed seen the misery of My people in Egypt. I have heard them crying out because of their slave drivers, and I am concerned about their suffering."*

The children of Israel had been in Egypt for over 400 years. During that time the Israelites had become slaves to the Egyptian people, and now the Egyptians were attempting to murder their male babies. The Israelites were suffering greatly at the hands of the Egyptians, and had been crying out to God for some time. It is not a good feeling to cry out and feel like no one hears you or can see your pain. This Scripture proves that God cares about our suffering and sees our pain.

There's Comfort in Knowing Someone Cares

When you are in misery, sometimes the only thing that can help is knowing somebody cares about your suffering. There is comfort in knowing somebody cares. The children of Israel had been suffering for a long time. These people were the descendants of Abraham, Isaac, and Jacob. Because of the stories told by their forefathers, they knew God had answered prayer before. During their captivity the Israelites cried out continuously for help, but God operates on a timetable that we humans do not always understand. We may question Him, but that does not mean He will alter His plan.

This Scripture comforted me as I continued my search to find out where God was when I cried. If you look closely at this Scripture in Exodus, it says God indeed saw their misery. He saw their misery even before He did anything about the pain.

Here's another Scripture that shows that God hears our cry:

For He has not despised or disdained the suffering of the afflicted one; He has not hidden His face from him but has listened to his cry for help (Psalm 22:24 NIV).

Sometimes we feel that no one cares, that no one has seen our pain. God says in this Scripture that He is concerned about our suffering. The New King James Version says in Exodus 3:7: "...for I know their sorrows." I like to know that God knows about my sorrows even if He does not answer my cry right then.

Remember, you are not alone in trying to sort this out. Many people before you have struggled and even now are struggling with the same issues. The first thing you need to do is to break the silence. Realize that you don't need to deal with your pain alone. If you are confused or angry, tell God right now how you feel. Remember, God will not punish you for being honest with Him about your feelings. Believe that the Lord hears your cry and wants to help you through your lonely silence.

Then you will call, and the Lord will answer; you will cry for help, and He will say: Here am I (Isaiah 58:9a NIV).

*   *   *

Holy Father, I am not sure how to ask You to help me. I have been quiet for so long. I am not sure how much I need help. I am not sure how much I hurt or even if I do hurt. I need You, Father, to help me untangle my feelings. I may be scared to feel. Help me have the courage to look at myself through Your eyes. Father, my silence may be from fear, from ignorance, or from a deep feeling of helplessness. Whatever it is from—or if I have been silent and do not even realize it— help me to open up to You and gain understanding and wisdom as I read. In Jesus' name. Amen.

Chapter 4

Uncovering Hidden Hurts

Surely You desire truth in the inner parts; You teach me wisdom in the inmost place (Psalm 51:6 NIV).

The human mind and all of its emotions are very complex. Often we don't seek help in dealing with emotional issues because we are not aware that we need help. We are not sure what the issues are in our lives. In my counseling practice, I find this is one of the biggest hurdles to get over. Many people have been wounded so deeply by their past that their feelings are numb. They cannot see how their past is affecting their present-day world. Yet, our unmet needs, which are rooted in the past, can and will control us. Understanding why we have these unmet needs is often the key to unlocking the motivating force behind certain actions.

Some of you may not realize that you are in emotional pain, but it's possible for people to have feelings inside that they don't know are there. You might not know your own heart, so you might not know what you really want or need. Recognize that you may have emotional injury that you are not aware of, and that you could need some help sifting and sorting your motives, desires, and needs.

One indication of having past wounds that you are unaware of is not understanding why you behave and react to certain things the way you do. For example, you may feel that your ability to relate to people or to express emotions is limited. Or, you may say, "I can be the greatest con artist in the world. Why do I con people?" You can make people believe almost anything and you use that ability for selfish gain. You know that there is something going on inside of you that does not please the Father, but you do not know what it is or what to do about it.

The Scriptures have helped me understand why we lack this knowledge. The Bible gives us the impression that the Lord is the only one who really knows our heart. Jeremiah 17:9-10 (NKJ) says, "The heart is deceitful above all things, and desperately wicked; who can know it? I, the Lord, search the heart, I test the mind...." However, the Bible also says that "if any of you lacks wisdom, he should ask God, who gives generously to all without finding fault, and it will be given to him" (Jas. 1:5 NIV). God knows that we do not always understand our hearts, but with His help we can unravel our thoughts and feelings.

You must seek wisdom and ask for God's help as you begin to look into your past. As you read this chapter, ask Him to show you any emotional wounds in your own life that have been ignored and left to fester, so that you can address them, free yourself from the bondage they created, and move toward healing.

Looking for Hidden Pain

Many things can happen that leave lasting and hidden effects on your inner being. But, since there is no way a book can review all the possible events, we'll just look at some general questions and strategies that can help you identify things that may be holding you in bondage.

In therapy sessions, I always ask my clients who affirmed them the most in their life. (*Affirm* means to express dedication, to validate.) Who made them feel valuable? Who taught them to be a man or a woman? I am always surprised at the number of people who answer honestly and say, "No one."

Generally much can be learned from that one question. Who encouraged you when the chips were down? Who let you know there was a better day ahead if you had a bad day? Who in your life believed in you? Who gave you unconditional love? If you never received unconditional love, you can be very performance-oriented. You feel that you must produce to be accepted.

I also ask, "Did you feel loved growing up?" I don't ask, "Were you loved?" but "Did you *feel* that you were loved?" Many parents love their children the best they can, but some children have never *felt* loved. Some good, caring parents are emotionally unable to communicate love to their children. Some children have difficulty receiving love. Regardless of the reason, if you did not feel loved when you were growing up, then you need to address this problem.

What If I Can't Remember?

I know there are people reading this who might say, "I am not sure how to verbalize my loss. I know that my childhood was not the best, but I cannot specifically say what the point of entry was for this pain I am feeling." Do not be discouraged. You may receive more revelation as you read. Just keep asking the Father to reveal anything that needs to be revealed for your complete restoration.

When you are a child and some type of severe emotional injury occurs, you may be too young cognitively to handle the situation. You may remember only that you felt bad. You may not actually remember the painful occurrence. We humans have the capacity to forget actual events but to remember the emotions that accompanied the event. These emotions sometimes surface for no apparent reason. We may not know why we are so scared in certain situations, but we know that we are. An example of this may be a child who was abused by a person wearing a red shirt. Later in life whenever that person sees someone wearing a red shirt he gets panicky and has no idea why. He has no actual memory of abuse, but his mind remembers the emotion that was present at the sight of the red shirt and triggers that emotion again.

It's okay if you can't remember the specific cause of the injury (though it is very helpful and worthwhile to try). The acknowledgment that something is wrong is the key. Once you admit, "I have something driving me on the inside—I am easily agitated; I am extremely moody; I am hard to get along with; I am sad too much of the time; I have a bad temper that needs some help"; you can then start asking God to reveal to you the emotional wound associated with that behavior.

Inherited Thinking

Up until this point I have discussed direct pain, or emotional trauma that affected you directly. However, you may have acquired hidden hurts "secondhand." Your parents could have experienced emotional pain and subsequently passed down to you the thought processes they developed because of their pain.

For example, if you have low self-esteem, but you do not have any memory of any specific trauma in your life, you could have possibly inherited that mind-set from one or both of your parents. They could have felt overcontrolled, unsupported, or unloved by their own parents during their childhood and may have never dealt with the pain. If your parents have always interpreted life through this mind-set of inferiority, they probably taught you to think in an inferior way. Thus, you might feel inferior but not know *why* you feel inferior.

Your parents could have experienced direct emotional trauma that made them feel shameful. If they did not work through their own injuries, they may have passed these feelings on to you as well. You have feelings of shame and you are not sure why. In reality, you're just responding to hidden hurt that you have unknowingly inherited.

Here are some more examples of unhealthy mind-sets or thought processes that you might have inherited and how they could affect you. You may have inherited a "give up" tendency if, as a child, every time you wanted to take on a difficult project your parents tried to talk you out of it because it was hard. You now have to stop your thought process and tell yourself that it is okay to work hard at a project.

The mind-set of laziness can be inherited. To break that mind-set you will have to deal with yourself, not your parents. They may remain in their mind-set, but that does not mean you cannot change.

Parents who were very fearful may have programmed you to be overly cautious. You may have difficulty walking in faith because you have had fear drilled into you all your life. This too can be overcome.

A parent who has a very cold personality and who always keeps people at a distance may have trained you to be distant toward other people. That does not mean you have to remain in that mind-set all your life. You can break free of mind-sets that are not good for you.

Hopefully you are beginning to realize that some of your pain and unhealthy thought and emotional processes could be inherited from your parents. Please don't be angry with them or blame them. They may not be aware of their own state of emotional being. They may not know how to free themselves from their pain.

Part of your healing is understanding that your parents had their pain too. This present generation is more open to talking about emotional pain than the one before us. The advent of television has brought many needed subjects to light. I am sorry that the Christian church has not taken the lead in trying to help people deal with disappointments. The daytime talk shows have forced the Christian community to deal with many issues that should have been dealt with first in the church.

You will never be totally healed until you deal with forgiveness—for your parents and others. Over the years, I have met people who feel that one should only forgive those who deserve forgiveness. The sad thing about that attitude is that no one deserves forgiveness. We are all like sheep who have gone astray; some have just wandered farther than others. "All we like sheep have gone astray; we have turned every one to his own way; and the Lord hath laid on Him the iniquity of us all" (Is. 53:6). I feel that this generation will be held more accountable than ever. We have the Bible on video, on computer software, and on audiotapes. We have many books that will help us deal with the past. We have many ways to seek wisdom. Jesus died for all—and that means He died for the people who have hurt you. Their sins are under His blood just like your sins are.

Gift of Forgiveness

I have heard some abuse stories that were so horrible that I have prayed and asked God to give the victim a gift of forgiveness. I felt that the people who were violated were so wounded that they would need help to be able to forgive. God understands your heart. He alone knows about your pain. If you ask, God will help you to forgive. Forgiveness is not an option; it is a command. Jesus tells us in Luke 6:37, "Judge not, and ye shall not be judged: condemn not, and ye shall not be condemned: forgive, and ye shall be forgiven." If you are having trouble forgiving, start by saying, "Lord, I want to be able to forgive. Please help me to be able to forgive."

When you are trying to discover and deal with an inherited mind-set, you need to ask the Lord to help you see the connection between your life and your parents' past. Once you are aware of pain that you've inherited, then you can seek healing for it just as you would any other type of pain.

What Are the Most Common Indicators of Hidden Pain?

There are many indicators that can reveal unresolved pain in your past. Here are just a few of the warning signs:

1. *Low Self-esteem*—You never feel quite good enough or valued or affirmed.

2. *Uncontrollable Anger*—You are easily irritated and sometimes feel a rage welling up within you that is disproportionate to the immediate and seeming cause.

3. *Emotional Insulation/Isolation*—You keep people at a distance by building nice thick walls around yourself. You insulate yourself emotionally because you think feelings are too expensive to risk.

4. *Workaholic Tendencies*—You need to be appreciated, respected, and valued, and working hard is the only way you know to get what you need.

5. *Inability to Trust*—You can't bring yourself to trust anyone.

6. *Comforting Yourself With Destructive Behaviors*—You can't seem to control yourself in areas such as eating, drinking alcohol, taking drugs, or having unhealthy and destructive relationships.

7. *Being a People Pleaser*—You desperately need the approval of others.

Why Is It Necessary to Bring Up Hurts From the Past?

When a person starts discovering things about himself that he never knew existed, he experiences a valuable release. It is hard to change when you do not understand what is wrong. Once a person starts to understand why he may have been emotionally closed to people all his life, then he has something to work on. When he realizes that fear has controlled him much of his adult life, he can begin to correct some of his faulty thinking.

We know from Psalm 51:6 (NIV) that God "desire[s] truth in the inner parts." The Holy Spirit will help you look deep inside yourself and see the truth. Ask God to reveal any pain that you do not know is present in your life. You don't experience pain just for the sake of hurting. No, whenever there is unvalidated pain, there is usually resentment—and resentment will keep you spiritually crippled. You do not want to be spiritually crippled. When you begin to see your pain and get validation for the wrong inflicted on you, there is a release. Jesus came to set the captives free.

* * *

Heavenly Father, I do not know how my childhood is influencing my behaviors today. I desire to know as much as You would have me to know. Father, whatever I need to see, please reveal it to me. Help me know my own heart. Help me to be willing to allow You, through Your Holy Spirit, to guide me into all truth. In Jesus' name I pray. Amen.

Chapter 5

Healing Begins: Realizing You Are Hurting

Heal me, O Lord, and I will be healed (Jeremiah 17:14a NIV).

"But I will restore you to health and heal your wounds," declares the Lord (Jeremiah 30:17a NIV).

You may already be very much aware of your past and you are shouting, "Yes, yes! I know I have injury. I hurt immensely because of the pain and losses in my childhood. So what am I supposed to do about it?"

Understand that the injury or pain that you've suffered is not your fault. You did not deserve such treatment. However, how you respond to your particular situation is your responsibility. Many of us have had difficult childhoods and have had people hurt us as adults as well. You must deal with the issues at hand. It is your responsibility now to respond to your needs and to reach out for help.

Maybe you are not sure what your needs are. As you progress, I believe that God will give you great insight into your specific needs. We are going to rely on Father God to aid us.

Getting in Touch With Your True Feelings

Give yourself permission to be a not-so-perfect person. Put aside any false pretenses that you may use to mask your pain and be a person who is real. You need to be able to say, "I hurt because I was sexually, physically, or emotionally abused as a child." "I hurt because no one loved me growing up." "I hurt because the person I trusted the most violated me." Or, "I hurt because I feel alone so much of the time now."

Give yourself permission to say, "I hurt." It's not your fault that you were mistreated, and it is not a sign of weakness to admit that you've been abused. Expressing your pain takes strength, but it is the first step in the healing process—a process that will eventually make you stronger by unloading the excess emotional baggage you've been carrying. Remember that when Lazarus died, Jesus wept (see Jn. 11:35). Jesus expressed His loss. There is something healing in expressing your pain.

Identify incidents and people who have betrayed and destroyed your trust, and realize that these may have made it difficult for you to trust anyone, including God. Your ability to love may be limited, not because you are an unlovable person, but because you have been wounded and have never been healed.

Sometimes it helps to write down how you feel and what hurt you. Be specific:

"I have hurt greatly because my parents over-looked me growing up."

"I hurt because I was violated at a young age."

"I do not feel anything when I think of my past. I do not feel good and I do not feel bad. I am numb."

"I hate my stepfather for abusing me."

"I hate my mother for not stopping the abuse."

"I do not know how to feel about God because I was hurt so badly growing up."

"My past has always haunted me."

"I want to feel better on the inside, but I don't know how to feel better."

"I don't know which way to turn to get help."

Grieving Involves Realizing What You Lost

It hurts to be taken advantage of, to be used, ig-nored, or violated. It hurts to lose a business, or to be betrayed by a business partner, a parent, a spouse, or a friend. The pain you feel is the result of the loss you ex-perienced. As mentioned in Chapter 2, "If you have a hole [in your soul], you suffered a loss." In order to deal with your past and move on, you must allow your-self to grieve your losses.

The first step in grieving involves acknowledging the loss. The second step requires you to verbalize your loss. The third step is to assess the damage. If you were abandoned either physically or emotionally by a parent or a loved one, then you lost security, comfort, and love. If you were abused by a parent, stepparent, or any other authority figure, then you lost trust and respect for authority. If you lost the right to be a child, then you lost a normal childhood. It was not your fault, and it hurts to be robbed of a part of you.

To help you acknowledge that there is a loss, pause for a moment. Shut your eyes and ask God to reveal your losses to you. Ask God to reveal to you the specific losses you experienced as a child that now are affecting your spiritual walk. Ask God to unclutter your mind so you can see clearly what is affecting you. Try to list your losses. Write them down on a piece of paper. Consider which (if any) of the following losses apply to you and add them to your list.

- loss of love and support
- loss of affirmation and self-esteem
- loss of discipline and guidance
- loss of consistency and normal family life
- loss of material possessions
- loss of parental approval
- loss of adult male or female companionship
- loss of a parent from death or separation
- loss of trust
- loss of security

Take the paper in your hand. Raise it up to the Lord and ask Him to heal that pain or that loss. Ask Him to make the pain stop hurting; ask Him to relieve the pressure; ask Him to lighten your load. God cares about your pain. He cares that you suffered. Ask Him to give you peace as you surrender all these emotions to Him.

The healing process that starts with verbalizing your pain and grieving your losses does not happen in an instant (unless God chooses to work a miracle). It may take some time, just as all grieving does. Often the longer you wait to address past hurts, the longer it takes for them to heal.

However, I want to warn you that some people can get stuck in grief. I do not want that to happen to you. Grief is a necessary step to your mental health, but you must pass through and come out of grief. Satan would love to see you stay in this step. Self-pity takes over when you stay in grief too long. You need to acknowledge the loss, to grieve, and to say that it hurts. Then you need to begin asking the Father for healing.

God is working in you today to bring healing to your heart. You *will* feel better.

* * *

Heavenly Father, I pray that out of Your glorious riches You will strengthen me with power through Your Spirit in my inner being, so that Christ may dwell in my heart through faith. And I pray that I, being rooted and established in love, may have power, together with all the saints, to grasp how wide and long and high and deep is the love of Christ, and to know this love that surpasses knowledge—that I may be filled to the measure of all the fullness of God. In Jesus' name I pray. Amen.

Ephesians 3:16-19 (paraphrased)

Chapter 6

Anger and Rebellion

Get rid of all bitterness, rage and anger... (Ephesians 4:31 NIV).

For man's anger does not bring about the righteous life that God desires (James 1:20 NIV).

Humans possess an amazing ability to cope with emotional pain. When we don't choose to deal with our emotions in a healthy way, our inner self finds some other way of dealing with the pain. Anger and rebellion are two of the most common and destructive manifestations of suppressed emotional pain.

There is a pattern that can develop when you are abused. You initially experience pain and hurt. You have been violated in some way. This pain causes holes in your soul. You are wounded, but it was not your fault and it doesn't seem fair. You need help but are unable to ask for it, so you hold it inside. You become angry because you've suffered a loss.

People are not born angry. Anger is a secondary reaction to an initial feeling of hurt. There is always pain behind anger. If that pain is not vented properly, the anger will build up. When you have unexpressed anger, you can become anxious, sad, rebellious, and depressed.

Anger has a way of becoming generalized and transferable. All of us have experienced being angry at ourselves and taking that anger out on our family or a close friend. You can have misdirected anger and not be aware of it. You may even direct anger toward God because you're unable to vent your anger toward the one who hurt you. You also may be unable to express your disappointment in God for allowing the hurt to happen.

Loss of Respect for Authority

Mistreatment affects a person's ability to trust and respect authority. If, as a child, you were taught to respect authority, but then an authority figure betrays you or violates you, you have a big problem. The issue of respect becomes messed up. How do you respect someone who treated you so badly? You become confused and angry.

Unexpressed anger can lead to rebellion against all authority figures. This inability to trust and respect authority can carry over to your relationship with the heavenly Father. People who have moved into rebellion have a special spiritual problem, because they refuse to or are unable to submit to Father God.

Rebellious people do not want to need anyone or anything. They want to handle all their problems on their own. They rebel against opening themselves up to any solution for their problems other than their own solutions.

Spiritual Significance of Rebellion

Rebellion is unique because it is a resistance to *any* authority. I want to help you understand the seriousness of this issue of rebellion. Rebellion interferes with your relationship with God. In the Bible rebellion was considered a serious transgression.

In First Samuel 15:22-23 (NIV), Samuel said rebellion was like divination. Divination means the foretelling of future events by supernatural means apart from God. In the Old Testament the Father was clear when He instructed Moses to tell the Israelites how He felt about them practicing witchcraft, sorcery, and the like: "Do not practice divination or sorcery" (Lev. 19:26b NIV).

You may be wondering what all that has to do with you and rebellion and God's authority. For one thing, God desires to be your source of information. He does not want you to be looking for guidance from other sources besides Him. However, when you think that you don't need anyone but yourself, you're valuing your own advice above any advice that you could receive from God. This is a form of rebellion against His authority.

Unintentional Rebellion

You may be in a position of unintentional rebellion and not realize you are there. You arrived there not by choice, but because the circumstances in your life caused you to be independent-minded. The relationship between independence and rebellion is important to understand. *Independence* means not being subject to control by others or not being affiliated with a larger controlling unit. *Rebellion* is a resistance to any authority. Whether you are resistant to authority or not subject to authority, you have a problem with submitting to the Holy Father's will. If this is the case, you will probably keep that position of independence and unintentional rebelliousness until something comes along in your life that you are powerless over, and which will make you begin to search for some answers. At that point, you'll take a hard look at your life and begin to realize that there is an authority higher than you.

Once you determine that there is a being higher than you and you accept God as that being, you should accept that His knowledge is not limited as is yours. This changes things. Once you accept Jesus and ask God to take over your life, you now have contact with a loving God who has all authority in Heaven and on earth.

Because of this new revelation, you now realize that things may not operate as you thought they did. God has ways of doing things that may be foreign to us. However, as we seek Him and see His ways unfold, we start realizing just how much we need His direction in our lives.

People who are rebellious toward authority in general may have trouble with God's directions simply because they are accustomed to following their own directions without question. They may believe that God is real, but they do not like God directing their lives.

When a person begins to allow God to direct his life, he realizes that he is not in control as much. This is hard for someone who has been on his own all his life. It's a whole new way of thinking.

You may be threatened by all this. You may be saying, "How can I submit to God when I have never submitted to anyone?" "How can I feel comfortable submitting to a Being I can't see or physically touch?" "How can I appreciate His sovereignty when I am so locked in this independent mind-set?" The sovereignty of God becomes a real issue. God's authority becomes a real problem for you.

In order to release this independent mind-set, you must take a spiritual journey. The way to stop being so independent is through the spirit. You must experience the Spirit of God. God's Spirit cannot be intellectualized. Intellectually, the mind will tell you to trust only yourself. The Spirit of God tells you to just try the Lord and you will see Him back you up. This trying is the leap of faith.

One of the hurdles that rebellious people must get over is accepting the fact that God has the right to design things as He chooses. A rebellious person may have difficulty accepting the salvation plan God has designed for us: God requires atonement for sin; atonement means reparation for a wrong; reparation means making amends for sin; sin means transgression of divine law. If a person has trouble accepting the Bible as God's divine message to us, then there is a real problem. The

Bible gives us God's Word. If a person does not interpret God's Word as divine, then he will have great trouble submitting to the teachings that the Bible relates to us.

Hope for the Angry Rebel

Humans are not born angry. You were not born rebellious. The anger and rebellion you struggle with developed over a period of time. You may not know how to vent your anger or even recognize that the anger is there, but it's important that you seek to understand why you have anger and why you are directing it as you are.

Realize that if you were abused by an authority figure, you may have difficulty with other authority figures, including God. Don't accept that difficulty as permanent!

Rebellious people are generally stubborn. Use that stubbornness for your own good. Realize that rebellion is a problem with your mind. To be rebellious, you must be hard and strong. Be hard and strong—but see that some of your convictions may be wrong.

In the past, you were convinced that you could count on no one but yourself. Realize that you can count on the Father. Be hard and strong in your persistence to hear the Father speak to you. Look at the gap between the Father and you and shout to the devil that your God is fighting for you! You will move straight into the Father's arms. Say, "God is over there and I am here, but not for long. With God's help I am crossing over."

Jesus Christ came to destroy the works of the devil (see 1 Jn. 3:8). The devil has come to rob, steal, and destroy your life if possible (see Jn. 10:10). A good Christian must be a good soldier, and good soldiers always follow their leader's instructions. Do not assume you know everything. Ask the Father to teach you His ways.

* * *

Father, please help me see the things in my life that have made me angry and rebellious. Help me know how to be less independent and more dependent on You. Show me where I am the most resistant to You. Father, help me to see Your strong desire to help me trust You. In Jesus' name. Amen.

Chapter 7

Comforting Ourselves With Unhealthy Responses to Pain

There is a way which seemeth right unto a man, but the end thereof are the ways of death (Proverbs 14:12).

Until the issues of rejection, abandonment, betrayal, and the like are dealt with properly, we attempt to deal with them in unhealthy ways. People who have been hurt, especially in childhood, build strong defense mechanisms in order to survive the severity of the abuse. Defense mechanisms are types of reactions we have that help us deal with conflict in our lives. These reactions are unconscious and are designed to bring stability or comfort to us. There are also things that we do consciously to comfort ourselves. However, while conscious comforts and defense mechanisms may serve a good purpose, they can also cause difficulties of their own.

Comforting Ourselves

When a person feels shaky physically or emotionally, he generally tries to make himself feel better. There is nothing wrong with wanting to feel better. We all need comfort at times throughout our lives. But people who experienced a childhood in which love was insufficient may seek to obtain comfort in ways that can be harmful.

I did some volunteer work last year in a homeless shelter. As I was praying through some of the teachings I was presenting there, the Lord showed me some things about our need for comfort. We know the Lord wants to comfort us because the Holy Spirit is described to us as the Comforter:

> *But the Comforter, which is the Holy Ghost, whom the Father will send in My name, He shall teach you all things, and bring all things to your remembrance, whatsoever I have said unto you* (John 14:26).

People will seek comfort. If they do not understand or have the strength to seek comfort in a constructive way, they will seek comfort in a destructive way. The homeless shelter experience helped me see that the need for comfort is much greater than I realized.

People search for comfort in a variety of ways, many of which are very unhealthy. Some destructive ways of seeking comfort include alcoholism, drug addiction, overeating, smoking, promiscuity, or abusive behavior. These behaviors comfort at first, but later lead to destruction.

Emotional pain causes a loss in a person's life. That loss creates anxiety and depression. The need for comfort becomes intense because you want the anxiety and depression to leave. People consciously and unconsciously look for relief (comfort). Destructive ways are the path of least resistance. Constructive ways involve dealing with the truth. The truth is camouflaged by our defense mechanisms. A person must have the strength to begin looking for the right solution. Destructive ways of finding comfort are temporary. Constructive ways are permanent.

It is like the man with a leak in his roof. The quick way to handle the problem is to put a pot under the leak. The more constructive way is to find out where the hole is and patch it.

When we do not know how to access constructive comfort, we find ourselves engaged in some of these destructive behaviors:

A functional addict comes in from a hard day's work. As he enters his home, he immediately heads for the alcohol supply. His nerves are on edge. He needs to console himself. Before he can interact with family members, he must have a few drinks for comfort.

A woman in a marriage that is not as fulfilling as she would like, takes things into her own hands and comforts herself by having an illicit relationship. She feels that her needs are not being met at home, so she plans a rendezvous to console herself.

A man with an obesity problem or with an eating disorder such as bulimia may have problems at work. On break, he eats for comfort or regurgitates for relief.

Pressure is on at school or work for the drug addict. His mind wants to take a break from reality. He becomes depressed. He has reason to be depressed: Things in his life are upside down and he doesn't know how to flip things back the right way. A quick fix would make everything feel better.

Learn How to Hurt Well

As you receive healing and understanding, there is another component you will need to walk in victory: the strength to be disciplined. Many times we have comforted ourselves so much that we do not hurt well. When you realize that your tolerance for emotional pain is low and that you enjoy comforting yourself, you must cry out to the Father to give you a double portion of His strength. Any time you break a habit, there is suffering involved.

Defense Mechanisms

Defense mechanisms are reactions we develop to help normalize life around us. They help a person deal with painful situations, but they also cause some problems. Some common defense mechanisms include repression, denial, and emotional insulation.

If you were reared in a chaotic, abusive family, your main defense mechanism may have been denial or emotional insulation. You just denied that things were as bad as they were because admitting the truth was more than you could handle. You developed walls of denial to help you feel better about your life.

For instance, your home life may have been very embarrassing, chaotic, and shameful because of an alcoholic parent. You built a defense mechanism of denial and presented an "everything's okay" face to the public. In reality, everything was not good at home. You presented an attitude that said you didn't care about what was happening at home, when in reality you cared very much. You felt helpless so you denied the situation to decrease your stress. Because of that necessary callous exterior, you generally did not allow yourself to express pain. You never gave yourself permission to say, "I hurt." Now you feel you must always be in control and handle whatever comes up. You have never cried out to the Father for help because you shut down emotionally.

When you were a young child and things happened to you, you might not have had the cognitive ability to figure out what happened. (*Cognition* is the mental process of knowing and becoming aware.) In short, you might not have been old enough to make a good judgment about what happened to you. Your awareness was limited simply because your mind was not mature enough to think everything through.

This is especially true in sexual abuse, and even more so when the perpetrator was an authority figure in your life. You may have felt that what was happening to you was not right. However, you were taught to respect authority figures, and if an authority figure violated you, you then became confused. When you are violated in any way, whether it is physical abuse, verbal abuse, neglect, abandonment, or being overcontrolled, you build walls to keep out as much of the pain as you can. You may repress all or part of the memories of the abuse. (*Repress* means to put down by force, to hold in by self-control, to exclude from consciousness.) Because you had no way of making sense of everything, you built a wall of denial to help reduce the emotional pain.

Many times, because you were a child when this abuse, neglect, or domination happened, the only thing you could do was build a mental wall around yourself. You may not have been able to remove yourself from the abuse because the violator was a parent, stepparent, etc. Therefore, you limited the pain as much as you could by shutting down emotionally.

Neutral Zone of "No Feelings"

When you shut down emotionally, you go into what I call a *neutral zone*. The neutral zone is a condition in which you stop feeling. You are numb. The neutral zone is where many people who suffered abuse as a child feel very comfortable. It is safe. You feel secure there because you have emotionally insulated yourself. You let no one in and you stay neatly tucked behind your invisible wall.

When you go into a neutral zone, you stop feeling. This zone may have been necessary as a child to help you survive the abuse. This ability to kick into neutral is a defense mechanism.

When you have been hurt by people you love, you start feeling that you cannot trust anyone. Therefore, you may emotionally insulate yourself from all people.

When you emotionally insulate yourself, you reduce your self-involvement on an emotional level and thus reduce the possibility of being hurt. This is very important when you have been deeply disappointed or hurt, because you may have decided that feelings are too precious to risk.

Emotional insulation creates problems, however. An example of this condition could be the inability to express love the way you want to. A wife who has been hurt by her husband may not be able to love him on the level she would like because she is afraid of being hurt again. A husband who has constantly reached out physically to his wife, only to be rejected or ignored, shuts down emotionally to her because he cannot bear the rejection. A young woman who, as a child, was raped by someone, now has great difficulty extending herself sexually to her husband. She has emotionally insulated herself to the point that she is unable to reach out to the one she loves the most. A person who was so dominated by his parents that he is determined no one will ever control him again, may keep his mate at an emotional distance because of his fear of control.

The Foundation of Most Walls Is Fear

We build walls as a response to fear and pain. Many people build walls of denial and emotional insulation to protect them from all the intruders in their lives. You do not want your feelings betrayed and plundered. You do not want to be hurt so you make a defensive move and seal yourself off. This is smart in one sense. It helped you survive emotional attack. You are all sealed off and no one can reach you or hurt you. As long as you don't ever want anyone to get close to you, you are in good shape.

The problem comes when you want an intimate relationship with someone. You may not be able to reach out and love anyone. You may have to love everybody at a distance. That causes real problems in marriage. In a marriage, emotional insulation keeps our emotions restrained. The emotions are there, but because of the insulation they are not allowed to manifest themselves. This insulation can destroy the very essence of a marriage.

Marriage is built on intimacy. *Intimacy* is defined as something of a personal or private nature. When you have walls around you, your deepest nature is not accessible to your mate.

For example, let's take a man who has been reared by a very controlling mother. His mother was the first invader. All he heard growing up were negative, critical comments about himself. This destroyed his self-esteem. His mother allowed very little deviation from her will. He had to do everything her way or the verbal assault would begin.

This man may feel emotionally enslaved to his mother. To survive this attack the man, as a young boy, built an emotional, fortified wall around himself. His mother may control his actions, but she will not control his heart, the most personal part of his being.

As a young boy he trusted his mother. It may have taken him quite a while to figure out that she was making controlling decisions when it came to his life. Therefore, in order for the young man to cope, he built a defensive wall and emotionally insulated himself from her.

At first it was just her. Later in life, he became confused about who would come in and plunder his goods (devalue him, degrade him) like Mom did, so he built another wall just in case some other person tried to control him. Now he felt safe and secure. No one could come in to move close to his heart. To secure his position, he stayed there behind the wall.

This young man grew up and met a beautiful, attractive woman. He desired to have a relationship with her. By now, his walls were a part of his personality and he presented himself as being very guarded. His new girlfriend also had many needs. She wanted to get married even though she knew he was a little distant. She felt that when they got married, everything would change.

It did change, but not the way she thought. When they married, she became more demanding because he kept her at a distance and she wanted that distancing to stop. She felt that since they were married, he should trust her.

When she asks, "Why don't you trust me?" he looks at her in dismay. He does not know what she is talking about because he is just like he was when she was dating him, and what else does she want?

As the wife's demands for intimacy increase, the husband feels threatened and fortifies his walls to keep out invaders. The husband is thinking, *Who knows, she may do to me what my mother did and try to control me, so I had better keep her at a distance.*

Another example of these neatly built walls could be a young woman who marries her high school sweetheart. During their courtship she too kept him at an emotional distance. He felt that when they got married, things would change. They did change—but not in the way he planned.

This young woman had been sexually abused as a child. She never told anyone. She endured the abuse by building walls that emotionally insulated her from the abuser. Now that she was experiencing pressure to become sexually intimate with her husband, she became even more distant.

This woman never resolved the pain and emotional injury she experienced as a child. She greatly distrusts everyone because she was violated as a child. Her husband does not understand why they are not becoming closer.

The young woman does not know how to separate the negative feelings she has for the abuser and the positive feelings she has for her husband. She loves her husband, but she is unable to express that love. She feels like she is in an emotional trap. She becomes confused. She becomes unable to separate these feelings. She handles this by emotionally insulating herself when it comes to intimacy and sexual relations. She has never learned how to release all this hurt and pain.

The two people I have described will often seek help from a marriage counselor. The presenting problem may be sexual incompatibility; however, in reality we have a person in great need of healing for abuse from childhood.

Walls are necessary to survive as a child, but they are fatal to keep as an adult. You can see that the walls the man built as a child helped him survive his mother's controlling force over him. Yet these same helpful walls are destroying his marriage. How does he learn to trust? How does he get healing for the initial trauma? How does he take down his walls and allow his wife to be close to his heart?

The walls that the woman built as a child helped her also survive the abuse. These same walls are now destroying *her* marriage. This woman has to ask the questions that the man asked. How does she get healing for her initial trauma? How does she learn to trust? How does she learn to take down her walls?

*   *   *

Father, help me realize the ways I have been comforting myself. Help me realize the unhealthy responses I am making. Reveal to me how this is interfering with my relationship with You. Father, send Your Holy Spirit to comfort me as I seek You. In Jesus' name. Amen.

Be confident of this,
I have begun a good work in you
and I will complete it!

Be Strong &
Have Courage!

J O S H U A   1 : 7

Chapter 8

Walls: Necessary to Survive But Fatal to Keep

Being confident of this very thing, that He which hath begun a good work in you will perform it until the day of Jesus Christ (Philippians 1:6).

If you have ever studied European history, you may remember how important the walled cities were. When you travel in Europe or the Middle East, you see that all the early cities were walled. They were surrounded by walls for protection from nomadic marauders. Marauders were rogues who were looking for an opportunity to plunder the cities. Therefore, the citizens of the cities built strong walls to keep out the invaders.

Fortress to Emporium

In order for a city to grow and progress in society, the lords of the city recognized the need to progress from a fortress to an emporium. An *emporium* is a place of trade, a place of business that serves customers like a shopping center. Good shopping centers need several things: easy access, merchandise to sell, and interaction between clerks and customers.

The merchandise we human beings have to sell is ourselves—our thoughts, our ideas, our feelings, our hopes, our dreams. Thus our emotional walls limit our access to people; they limit our interaction with people we love or want to love. What does that have to do with emotional injury?

The early cities had to build walls to keep out invaders. You may feel that you have been invaded and plundered emotionally. You may feel defenseless, helpless, and alone. You may have had to build emotional walls around yourself to survive your day-to-day life, but when you build walls, you limit the access other people have to you, as well as the access you have to other people.

Walled cities completely dictated when people could do business and when they could not. It was not a mutual relationship. It was a relationship totally dependent upon when the gates in the walls were opened. Similarly, in a husband-and-wife relationship or a father-and-son relationship, for real communication to occur, the one with the invisible walls has to take the initiative to open the gates.

Some of you today may feel that you have been conquered and plundered. The walls you have built limit who can interact with you on a meaningful level. Your access to your family may be limited and your family's access to you is definitely limited. In addition, your neatly built walls limit your closeness to God.

You must understand that God has the power and the ability to take down your walls. God has the power and authority to heal you of every childhood pain you have ever experienced. God cares about your broken heart. In Psalm 34:18 (NIV) the Psalmist said, "The Lord is close to the brokenhearted and saves those who are crushed in spirit." People may feel crushed by their painful experiences. This Scripture tells us that God wants to save those crushed in spirit.

Also in Psalm 147:3 (NIV) the Psalmist says, "He [the Lord] heals the brokenhearted and binds up their wounds." God wants to bind up your wounds.

God gave that power and authority to our Lord and Savior, Jesus Christ. Look in Luke 4:18 (NIV), where Jesus is reading from the scroll of Isaiah about Himself:

> *The Spirit of the Lord is on Me, because He has anointed Me to preach the good news to the poor. He has sent Me to proclaim freedom for the prisoners and recovery of sight for the blind, to release the oppressed.*

Taking Down the Walls

Fear is the foundation of most walls. Dislodging this fear can be quite simple, but also extremely hard. The Bible says in Second Timothy 1:7, "For God hath not given us the spirit of fear; but of power, and of love, and of a sound mind." In First John 4:18 (NIV), John says, "There is no fear in love. But perfect love drives out fear, because fear has to do with punishment. The one who fears is not made perfect in love."

What are you afraid of? Do you even know? Ask the Father to reveal to you today what your deepest fear is. Ask Him to help you understand why you have built and now keep your walls. He wants to help you be the person He created you to be. He waits only for your invitation to begin the recreating process.

How do you remove the emotional threats you carry around? The first thing you have to do is be honest with yourself and say, "I have felt threatened much of my life and I am not sure I want to change now." You have to begin to realize that with Father God's help you are more powerful than the threats you have been fearing. You have to gain the assurance that you can handle the emotional invaders. This will be a whole new thought process for you. You will feel yourself changing as you allow the Father to take down your walls.

As just stated, to take down your walls you have to have assurance that you can handle the next invaders. That total assurance comes from a personal relationship with Jesus Christ. Jesus Christ is the key to your locked gate. He must become the commander-in-chief of your army to keep out the invaders.

Lord, I Need to Know That You Will Back Me Up If I Lower My Walls

In the past, your walls have been keeping the invaders out. Now, your strategy must change. The presence of the Lord Jesus and His precious Holy Spirit become your defense. Therefore, you must have complete confidence in the Lord's ability to see you through. You must know, that you know, that God is everything you need.

God told Moses that He is the I am. "God said to Moses, 'I AM WHO I AM...' " (Ex. 3:14 NIV). This must mean something to you in order for God to be your security. God must be viewed as valuable. God must be viewed as having unlimited capabilities. You must see God as a living, active, caring God.

There are more than ten different meanings of the word for "God" in the Bible. I want to show you how powerful they are. *El-Shaddai* means Almighty God. *Adonai* means the Lord, which signifies ownership. *Jehovah-jireh* means the Lord will provide. *Jehovah-rophe* means God heals. *Jehovah-nissi* means He is my banner. *Jehovah-M'Kaddesh* means the God who sanctifies. *Jehovah-shalom* means the God of peace. *Jehovah-tsidkenu* means the Lord of righteousness. *Jehovah-rohi* means He is my shepherd. *Jehovah-shammah* means the God who is there.

He is there with you now as you read this book. He is the supplier of whatever your need is. He, Father God, is your protector. You must be able to see how mighty and powerful God is or this part will not be effective. If you are having trouble seeing this, please pray right now for God to open your eyes to the truth about Him. Also, bind the devil from influencing your mind. Just say, "In Jesus' name, I bind you, devil, from blocking the full understanding I need. I command you to leave my mind and heart right now."

After you have this assurance in your mind that Father God is able to protect you, you need to move to the next step.

Deliver Me, Lord, From the Need to Control

Another hindrance to taking down your walls is the issue of control. Be willing to ask God to deliver you from that need. When you start yielding to the Father and He starts rearranging your desires and motives, you lose control. When you allow the Father's thoughts, attitudes, motives, and desires to control you, you are no longer running the show. The Father, through His Holy Spirit, becomes the director and producer of your life. When you are free from your old mind-sets, you then become open for business—God's business. You can do business for the Father in your family, your community, and your workplace.

Accepting Christ is the beginning. Just as God told Moses that He would lead the children of Israel out of bondage, so God is telling you that He will lead you out of your bondage of hurt. Moses had to continually listen to the Lord to receive His instructions. The same is true for you. God has much to share with you about yourself.

Living for the Lord is a journey. Just as Moses had problems to overcome on his journey, you will have problems to overcome on your journey. Sometimes *you* are the problem; sometimes other people are the problem. Taking down walls is difficult. Leaving Egypt was difficult for Moses. Leaving your past behind may be difficult, but you must be courageous. You will need to be encouraged by godly friends. You will have obstacles to overcome, but you are not alone. You have the Holy Spirit to guide you. As you lower your walls and allow God to give you understanding, you will feel stronger.

During the transition you may enter into what I call a *blank area*. The blank area is when you do not know who you really are because you have lowered your walls. You are very afraid of this area. You feel that if you change that part of your personality, you won't know who you are. You think that if you let go of your walls of pride, denial, perfectionism, and emotional insulation, then you will be exposed not only to the heavenly Father, but also to others. You are fearful that others may cause you harm. That is when you must be able to trust the Father. The thought of not knowing who you are for a season is frightening. It keeps many Christians from responding completely to God.

In this blank area you are depending on the Father to protect you instead of on your defensive walls. You have allowed the Father to start interacting with you through the Holy Spirit. You have trusted Him enough to entertain the thought of changing, but you do not know how to change because your whole life has been built on what you could do by yourself. You have to risk the control you have always cherished in order to allow the Father to reveal to you His strength. His strength in turn will strengthen you.

God does not want to make us weaker; no, God wants to make us stronger. God is a warrior (see Ex. 15:3). No one wants to go backward and become more vulnerable. We must see that the final result of lowering our walls is to eventually become stronger.

Walls come down when threats are decreased. Threats are decreased when healing occurs to the initial injury and understanding comes. Fellowship with

God brings strength. God's strength becomes our strength. Strength helps us decrease the threat.

A New Person Emerges

Once you start allowing your walls to be removed, you quickly realize that you are not the person you used to be. The walls were a part of your personality; now they are gone. This is a frightening thought.

Because the walls are gone, you do not react the way you always have. How are you going to feel comfortable allowing people to get close to you? How are you going to feel when you have always held a particular point of view, but now you realize that you must pray about this issue before you respond?

It is frightening to submit your thoughts and reactions to the Father. Sometimes you may feel blank, that you are just unsure. Your old scripts, which have told you how to act for so long, must be rewritten with the help of the Holy Spirit. (A script is a previous experience that you have stored away in your mind for future reference.) You must be willing to be uncomfortable until you start seeing yourself as confident. You now have to allow the Holy Spirit to teach you who you are in the Lord.

You can find assurance in the fact that the Father is in the process of teaching you who you are. You do not have to know it all. You can be at peace knowing that you are in the process of changing and that the Father will be faithful to complete this work in you. Philippians 1:6 says, "Being confident of this, that He who began a good work in you will carry it on to completion until the day of Christ Jesus" (NIV).

Learning to Trust

Trusting may be foreign to you. You built walls because of a lack of trust. You may have felt that you were not sure who you could trust...and that may be true. Now you realize there must be a shift in your attitude about trust.

What Does It Mean to Trust?

Trust is generally defined as reliance on the integrity of a person, or on some quality or attribute of that person. Trust is also defined as a condition of being committed into another's care or guarding. These definitions show that if you are trusting the Father, you have entrusted yourself to His care. Your being is confided to His care.

Trust implies a feeling of security. It is hard to trust when you have been plundered, used, and abused. What we are looking at now is moving from a closed attitude to an open attitude.

Threats Must Be Eliminated

Remember the example of the fortified city and the emporium? An emporium is a place of trade, a place of business that serves customers. Fortified cities were necessary when the possibility of attack was great. When the city wanted to be an emporium, the city had to decrease the feeling of threat from the outside and open itself up for trade. The threats had to be eliminated because the people needed to do business.

Some of you need to do business with your family, with your spouse, and with Father God. However, you may be so fortified emotionally that you have not been able to enter into a meaningful relationship. The threat of enemies from the past may have paralyzed you emotionally, and you are afraid to remove your walls.

Lord, Heal Me

You will need healing from that initial attack. Remember, Father God is *Jehovah-rophe*, the God who heals. You need to be able to verbalize your pain. You need to grieve briefly over your childhood. Next, you need to ask the Father to give you a revelation of how much Jesus loves you and how much the Father loves you. You need to see yourself as a valuable possession of the Father. You may not feel very valuable or very worthy. Part of this change that needs to happen in you is in your attitude about yourself.

You need a revelation of how strong you are in the Lord. You need to begin realizing that you do not have to fight the invaders alone. You have to see yourself handling the situation without shutting down. Taking down the walls without the assurance that you are not out there alone will not work.

Lord, Help Me Trust You

The hard part about all this is allowing the Lord Jesus to take control of your life. Letting Him lead you may be difficult if your ability to trust has not improved. You may not feel like you know who you are. The old you, when threatened, will shut down and withdraw. The new you will have to ask the Father, "How do we handle this situation from this point forward?" As you experience more and more of the

Lord's presence, you will have more and more confidence that you can handle the invaders in life.

Your walls come down when the threat is decreased. The threats are decreased when you feel strong enough to handle the attacks instead of running away and shutting down. You feel strong when you start understanding God and how much He loves you. You start understanding God when you start desiring His ways.

Respect and Trust Are Mutually Dependent

It is important to understand that you will not desire God's ways until you respect and trust Him. That respect must include a positive attitude toward the Father's authority. Very often, however, respect for authority is lost because trust is lost. Sometimes this loss of trust is very specifically related to abuse at the hands of those to whom we have given authority in our lives, or of those who naturally have authority over us, such as our parents. With this specific loss of trust comes a more basic loss of trust that can develop into a lack of respect for authority in general.

If you have trouble respecting authority or trusting anyone, including God, you have to explore why. Respect and trust are built on one another. You will not learn to respect God until you learn to trust Him.

God wants you to trust Him. Trust implies a feeling of security. It involves committing yourself into another's care. That is not usually done, however, unless you first believe that the person has your best interest in mind and will work for your good.

If you are not trusting God, then you are doubting that He will work for your good if you submit to His authority over your life. You have reservations about Him.

You may be saying, "I am still not sure I know how to trust the Father." Learning to trust is just like anything else you are learning to do for the first time. Your first try at trusting is almost like you are testing the Lord to see if He will be there for you. You may feel that you do not have the right to test the Father. However, God invites you in the Bible to test Him. Think about the following Scripture and see how it relates to this thought about testing the Lord. (The King James Version uses the word *prove* rather than the word *test* in this Scripture.)

> *"Bring the whole tithe into the storehouse, that there may be food in My house. Test Me in this," says the Lord Almighty, "and see if I will not throw open the floodgates of heaven and pour out so much blessing that you will not have room enough for it"* (Malachi 3:10 NIV).

God was inviting the people to put Him to the test. God was saying to give money to His work and see if He did not bless greatly. God did not say He *might* bless; He said He *would* bless. It is interesting to me that the Lord invited the people to try Him.

I am inviting you throughout this book to try the Lord. When you give God your trust, He will reward you with a blessing so great that you will have trouble containing it. You must begin somewhere in the trusting issue. This is the core issue. When I see people having difficulty trusting, it is as if there is a gulf between them and God. You will have no trouble believing God is sovereign if you trust Him.

On the Road to Trusting

Trusting a Being you do not see is not a natural thing. You must realize that trusting is a spiritual move on your part. Operating in the spirit is a leap of faith. Trusting requires that you change your mind-set. You must shift gears from your way to God's way.

Trusting requires listening to your thought processes. If you are trusting God, you are listening to the Father, not to all the other thoughts that try to invade your mind.

In trusting, it helps to know how God helped other people. That builds trust. This is why testimonies are so effective and powerful in churches. They are faith-building.

Trust requires you to say something to God. God is there and He is listening to you. You must at least say, "God, help me to trust You." You must begin a conversation with the Lord.

Trusting is like anything else new. You must learn to do it. It is like a baby learning to walk. A baby will never get off the floor and walk unless he first makes the attempt to move. Be like the man in Mark 9:24 when he asked Jesus to help his unbelief.

Your first attempt may not be successful. Do not give up. Remember how babies learn to walk. In the beginning they take a small step and fall down. Then they get up and try it again. So it goes with us as we learn to trust. We must try until we see the Lord's presence moving in our lives.

Trusting means we allow God to take control of our lives. Many times the issue of not trusting revolves around the issue of control. People know to cry out to God for help for their unbelief, but they do not do so. Why? They are afraid. They fear what He might lead them to do when He *is* there and He *does* answer. The issue is not that they do not know how to trust or listen; the issue is they do not want to yield their lives to the Father.

In the final analysis the question is, will you be able to let go of your free will? God does not take your free will. He lets you choose Him or reject Him.

God has always protected our free will. We voluntarily give Him our will when we trust Him. God wants us to be able to choose Him with no persuasion other than our own choice to do so. We voluntarily and consciously say to ourselves, "I trust the Father to lead my life. I intentionally give the Father the open door to my heart and my mind. I yield my will to the Father."

Free to Love

When your walls are down, you are free to love and be loved. What a sense of freedom to be able to love the people you have always wanted to love!

Now, you are free to allow the Father to start teaching you His ways. Ask the Father to make your life's experiences something that will strengthen you and not destroy you. Maybe you have never known how to love without selfish motivation. Maybe most of your love has been out of manipulation. Maybe you have been

afraid to let anyone get close to you. That's
day is a new day and you can shout to the   ...,
"Teach me Your ways, Lord. Teach me Your ways!"
Say to the Father, "I trust that You have a good plan
for my life." Look in Jeremiah 29:11 (NIV):

> *"For I know the plans I have for you," declares the
> Lord, "plans to prosper you and not to harm you,
> plans to give you hope and a future."*

*   *   *

*Holy Father, taking my walls down may be the hardest thing
I have ever done. Father, give me an understanding of You
that will increase my faith. Instead of running from this
process in my life, help me to run to You for help. Once I am
assured that You are completely with me, show me how to
think. Let my relationship with You be a confident relationship. Give me a great hunger for understanding and truth
about myself. In Jesus' name, I pray. Amen.*

I have strayed

like a lost sheep...

Seek your servant.

For I have not forgotten your commands.

PSALM 119:176

Chapter 9

Yielding to the Father Even When You Are Hurting

…nevertheless not as I will, but as Thou wilt (Matthew 26:39b).

Changing may be a new feeling for you, and anything new is a little scary. This scary zone is part of the process of changing. Changing is hard. No one likes to change. Please do not run from this part of the process. Allow the Holy Spirit to give you courage.

Our heart may be ready for the change, but our flesh is not. As we work on this process we have to remember Nehemiah's instruction to his people when they were under attack. Nehemiah knew the people had to keep on working, yet be willing to stop and fight when necessary. "…Those who carried materials did their work with one hand and held a weapon in the other, and each of the builders wore his sword at his side as he worked…" (Neh. 4:17-18 NIV). We are the same way. We must understand that while we are attempting to change, the enemy will attempt to abort our mission. This state of transition is not easy, but we can make it. Knowing as much of God's Word as possible will equip us to fight and persevere. We can also be encouraged by the stories of how others before us fought and won.

Courage is an interesting word. It is defined as mental or moral strength to venture, persevere, and withstand danger, fear, or difficulty. You would think that once you have courage you will always have courage. I believe the Word of God tells us that there are times we will need to be reminded to be courageous. Look at this passage in Joshua:

> *"Be strong and courageous, because you will lead these people to inherit the land I swore to their forefathers to give them. Be strong and very courageous. Be careful to obey all the law My servant Moses gave you; do not turn from it to the right or to the left, that you may be successful wherever you go. ... Have I not commanded you? Be strong and courageous. Do not be terrified; do not be discouraged, for the Lord your God will be with you wherever you go." ..."Only be strong and courageous!"* (Joshua 1:6-7,9,18 NIV)

Joshua was told four times in that one chapter to be strong and courageous. Why would Joshua have to be told this? Had he not seen enough that he would be strong and courageous all his life? Yet, even Joshua had to be reminded to be courageous. Let's look a minute at Joshua's life.

At this point in Joshua's life, Moses had just died. Joshua had been a faithful servant to Moses. He had been an eyewitness to some astounding miracles: the parting of the Red Sea; the daily provision of manna from Heaven; the sending of quails to provide meat for the children of Israel; and the plagues God sent on Pharaoh, to name a few.

You would think that he would never have to be reminded to be courageous. After all, Joshua and Caleb were the only two spies who believed that God would give the promised land to the children of Israel. (If you do not know this story, read Numbers 13–14.)

Joshua and Caleb were very upset when the other ten spies showed such a lack of faith that they convinced the Israelites not to enter the promised land.

Joshua son of Nun and Caleb son of Jephunneh, who were among those who had explored the land, tore their clothes and said to the entire Israelite assembly, "The land we passed through and explored is exceedingly good. If the Lord is pleased with us, He will lead us into that land, a land flowing with milk and honey, and will give it to us. Only do not rebel against the Lord. And do not be afraid of the people of the land, because we will swallow them up. Their protection is gone, but the Lord is with us. Do not be afraid of them" (Numbers 14:6-9 NIV).

At this point in his life Joshua demonstrated great courage. However, when Joshua replaced Moses, he still had to be reminded to be strong and courageous.

Perhaps at a young age you knew God and followed Him faithfully, but now you need to be reminded to be strong and courageous. As you deal with the walls you have constructed around yourself just to survive, you are going to have to be courageous.

Fear steals our courage. A new way of thinking makes us shaky. Changing mind-sets, attitudes, or opinions that you have clung to for most or all of your life is not easy. I want to exhort you to be strong and courageous as you search out those areas of your life that need to change.

Struggling With Right and Wrong

We all struggle with right and wrong no matter what our background is. When we are hurting, however, we may especially struggle to yield to the will of the Father. Sometimes we simply cannot choose right and do the Father's will unless the Lord fights for us.

Many Christians before us have struggled and won. They learned to die to self and endure the suffering and change that making the right choice and doing the right thing often involve. We need to examine their lives and the struggles they endured to see what we can learn from their experiences. In this way the lessons they learned can help equip us for the fight. The lives of the people that we are going to discuss demonstrate the necessity of seeking the Father's will and following it even when it is a struggle to do so.

Others Before You Have Struggled

I have been encouraged over the years by several people in the Bible who struggled with right and wrong. My favorite people are Paul, Moses, David, Jonah, and Peter.

Paul

Paul wrote much about struggling with right and wrong. Romans 7:7-25, in particular, addresses the issue of struggling with sin. At times, I find myself struggling much like Paul. Paul was not struggling with what was right and what was wrong; he was struggling with how not to do what he knew was wrong.

Romans 7:15 (NIV) tells us that he did not always do the right thing: "I do not understand what I do. For what I want to do I do not do, but what I hate I do."

The next verse shows that Paul understood the value of God's law—that it was a good thing and not bad. Paul said, "And if I do what I do not want to do, I agree that the law is good" (Rom. 7:16 NIV).

Paul was not suffering from a lack of understanding what is right and what is wrong. He understood. His problem was choosing to obey. *Knowing* what is right doesn't always translate into *choosing* it.

This past year I volunteered for six months, one day a week, in a homeless shelter. One thing I quickly learned was that the men understood that many of their choices had been bad choices. They did not need anyone to preach to them about what a bad choice is.

We humans willingly make many bad choices. We need to be taught how to choose right. Part of that teaching must deal with what to do when our heart is not right. Sometimes we enjoy holding grudges. Sometimes we enjoy talking about people. Sometimes we enjoy sinning. The Bible even gives the impression that sin may be enjoyable for a season. Hebrews 11:25 (NIV) says, "He chose to be mistreated along with the people of God rather than to enjoy the pleasures of sin for a short time."

This Scripture was referring to Moses. Moses could have remained in the Egyptian royal family; instead, he chose to be mistreated and to be faithful to his family.

Moses Struggled to Obey God

If you do not know the story of Moses as told in the Book of Exodus, the following is a quick synopsis for you.

Exodus tells how Moses was born at a time when the Israelite people had been enslaved by the Egyptians for quite some time. During their time in Egypt, the Israelites grew in number. Pharaoh, fearing them, wanted to decrease the population of the Israelites. He felt that one of the best ways was to eliminate the newborn male babies, so He instructed all the midwives to kill all Hebrew male babies.

Jochebed, Moses' mother, made the decision to hide her male baby to protect his life. She placed young Moses in a basket sealed with pitch, then put the basket in a river. Moses' sister, Miriam, stood watch at a distance. Baby Moses was discovered by Pharaoh's daughter. Thus Moses was reared as an Egyptian, the grandson of Pharaoh. Moses could have enjoyed all the pleasures he wanted.

When Moses was around 40 years old, he went out to see the Hebrew people work. While he was watching, he saw an Egyptian mistreat a Hebrew. In anger Moses killed the Egyptian. Moses left Egypt at that time and fled to Midian, where he stayed for 40 years. God spoke to Moses while he was in Midian. This was the burning bush account in which God told Moses to go back to Egypt and lead God's people out of their bondage.

Earlier in this book I mentioned the account of the Israelites crying out for help. Moses did not have to get involved in their pain. It would have been much easier to stay in Midian. But God called Moses for a special task. I am sure that Moses struggled at times in submitting to this call. If you read the first few chapters of Exodus you will see his struggle.

By the time God's call came, Moses was feeling quite displaced. He had been reared in the Egyptian royal household, but he was an Israelite. The Scriptures indicate that Moses must have looked very much like an Egyptian, for while he was in Midian he met some young women at a well. They went home and told their father that an Egyptian had helped them: "They answered, 'An Egyptian rescued us from the shepherds. He even drew water for us and watered the flock' " (Ex. 2:19 NIV).

Moses looked like an Egyptian and talked like an Egyptian, but he was not an Egyptian. What a case of not fitting in. Moses gave God several reasons why he was a poor choice to lead the Israelites out of bondage. Moses first said, "...Who am I, that I should go to Pharaoh and bring the Israelites out of Egypt?" (Ex. 3:11 NIV)

His Israelite people did not even know him. His Egyptian people felt betrayed by him. Thus it is not surprising that Exodus 3:11 reveals that Moses felt unworthy and questioned his ability to lead the people out of Egypt.

Next, Moses said to God, "...Suppose I go to the Israelites and say to them, 'The God of your fathers has sent me to you,' and they ask me, 'What is His name?' Then what shall I tell them?" (Ex. 3:13 NIV)

Then Moses complained to God that he was not a good orator. God sent Aaron to speak for Moses. But Moses was still looking for some way out of doing the right thing. In Exodus 4:1 (NIV), Moses said, "...What if they do not believe me or listen to me and say, 'The Lord did not appear to you'?"

This sounds like a legitimate concern to me. Moses is feeling very displaced. Moses is thinking, "I am an Israelite, but I look like an Egyptian and talk like an Egyptian. Now I am living in Midian with the Midianites."

I believe that Moses' poor self-esteem and fear still had such a grip on him that he could not see himself completing this task. God knew that Moses needed help. Therefore He supernaturally intervened to build up Moses' self-confidence. God gave him a miraculous rod, thus showing him that He was going to back him up.

Moses struggled with doing the right thing. He really wanted God to find someone else. Moses surely did not imagine that thousands of years later we would use him as an example of being obedient to the Father. All Moses knew was that there were many Israelites, and this promised land was a long way off.

Moses kept coming back with excuses until God's anger burned against him. God told Moses that Aaron, his brother, was already on the way to meet him. I am sure that this was another supernatural sign from God to encourage Moses and to show him that God would be with him.

Some of you may feel today that you have pushed God to the point of being angry at you. However, God said He is very long-suffering toward us. Nehemiah 9:17 says that God is slow to anger. You have to settle in your mind that you are not too far gone for God to help.

I regularly counsel people. Sometimes people come to me feeling that God won't be able to forgive them because their sins are so great. It is as if they have determined what God can and cannot handle, and their determination is that God will never be able to forgive them. I tell them that they cannot determine the long-suffering of God. As long as they are still interested in God, He is interested in them.

Jonah, Another Example of Struggling

Jonah was another person who resisted doing the right thing. His story is told in a short Old Testament book that is just four chapters long. Jonah was told by God to go preach against a city named Nineveh. Nineveh, which was located near present-day Iraq, was the capital of the Assyrian empire. Thus the book opens with the Lord saying to Jonah: "Arise, go to Nineveh, that great city, and cry against it; for their wickedness is come up before Me" (Jon. 1:2).

Jonah did not like his assignment. He did not like the people in Nineveh, probably because they were Gentiles. Consequently he saw no real use in helping them avoid the wrath of God. Instead of obeying the Lord, Jonah decided to catch a boat and go the opposite way. He went to the seaport of Joppa and there boarded a boat to Tarshish.

While enroute to Tarshish, Jonah was thrown overboard during a fierce storm and was swallowed by a big fish. After three days in the belly of the big fish, he rethought God's instructions. When the fish spit him out onto land, he went to Nineveh and preached against the Ninevites as God had instructed him. Jonah proclaimed that unless the Ninevites repented, the Lord would destroy them within 40 days.

Jonah was not happy when the people received his message and repented. What a story of human nature! He just did not like the people.

Aren't we like that sometimes? We resist doing the right thing simply because we do not really like the right way. Sometimes we get ourselves into a situation just as serious as Jonah's in the belly of the big fish. We resist doing what we know is right and end up in a situation that is every bit as devastating as the one Jonah found himself in. And like Jonah, we may become angry at God when things don't turn out like we want them to.

Jonah was not happy that God's compassion extended to all people. Jonah was a Hebrew prophet. He was a man of God. Still he struggled greatly to do the right thing.

Peter

Now let's look at Peter. Peter's story certainly reveals the pain we suffer when we resist doing the right thing.

One of the first disciples, Peter became a close friend of Jesus. In fact, he was the disciple who recognized Jesus as the Messiah (see Mk. 8:27-29). However, Peter also denied Jesus three times. Each of the four Gospels records Peter's denial of Jesus. (See Matthew 26:69-75; Mark 14:66-72; Luke 22:55-62; John 18:16-18,25-27.)

Peter knew that Jesus was the Messiah. Peter knew that denying Him was wrong, but he did it anyway. Jesus had even warned Peter that he would deny Him. At the time when Jesus predicted what was going to happen, Peter did not believe His prediction (e.g., Mt. 26:34-35). This is another lesson in human nature. How many of us have been warned and have continued in a sin anyway? How many of us have loved God and have continued in a sin anyway?

Peter's story has a great ending. After His resurrection, Jesus appeared on earth for 40 days. During that time He appeared to Peter and commissioned him three times to feed His sheep (see Jn. 21). Thus Peter was restored. He had repented and was forgiven. Yes, Peter struggled; but he did not give up.

Jesus, Our Precious Savior,
Struggled With Doing the Right Thing

The last person I want to discuss in this chapter is Jesus. I believe that Jesus, although He made the right decision, struggled with doing the right thing. He did not want to die, but He knew that He was going to have to die. If Jesus had wanted to die, I do not believe His sweat would have been like drops of blood (see Lk. 22:44) when He prayed three times on the Mount of Olives for this cup to pass from Him (see Mt. 26:36-44).

Nor would He have told His disciples, "...My soul is overwhelmed with sorrow to the point of death. Stay here and keep watch with Me" (Mt. 26:38 NIV).

Jesus struggled with doing the right thing, but He made the right choice. He was tempted as we are, but He was without sin (see Heb. 4:15). He was overwhelmed with sorrow, but He still accepted His Father's will and plan. All this cost Jesus much. He had to give up His friends and His family to do the right thing.

Sometimes we have to give up people we care about to be able to do the right thing. Sometimes we have to give up substances we care about to do the right thing. Sometimes we may be overwhelmed with sorrow as we choose the right thing. Doing the right thing does not always feel good. Doing the right thing may hurt for a while. Doing the right thing may be the hardest thing we have ever done.

Nevertheless, you can choose to do the right thing. Jesus sweated blood-like drops to do the right thing. You too may suffer and feel sorrowful as you make the choice to give up drugs, alcohol, gambling, an ungodly relationship, a negative attitude, gossiping, pride, or selfishness. Don't feel alone! You can tap into the same courage that sustained Jesus. Courage overwhelms the fear that keeps you from changing. It says that you can make it.

Sometimes we know what to do, we just need the courage to do it. Doing the right thing takes deep courage. We also need to be told that doing the right thing does not always feel good. It's okay to hurt. It's okay to be sorrowful. Things will get better.

Once a bad habit or thought pattern is established, the only way to break it is through discomfort. If we persistently avoid the pain, we keep delaying the freedom of being delivered from the control of the habit, addiction, or obsession. Therefore, we must realize that doing the right thing may be and probably at times will be uncomfortable and painful.

My Own Personal Struggle

There have been times when I have known that my heart was not right. During those times I have experienced many emotions as I tried to come to grips with the reality of where God was while I struggled. If I was committed to God, how could I desire to do something that is directly opposite to His law?

Often I questioned my commitment to God. I felt a sense of agony knowing that God loves me, yet having to decide whether or not I was going to obey Him. I wondered why I had to agonize over the decision whether or not to obey the Lord if I was truly in love with Him. Knowing that I love the Lord, how could I possibly be in a position in which I was willing to compromise my faith and commitment to God?

During those times of my life, I pressed into God harder than I ever had before. I had much trouble believing that a person could love God so much but be tempted so greatly. I prayed to God to let my love for Him increase to the point that I would love Him more than anything else and that my love for Him would be a natural deterrent to sin. I told the Lord, "I want to serve You and honor You because I love You, not because I am afraid You are going to send me to hell." It was in these times that I realized how weak my love for the Father was.

Your Definition of Love May Be Weak

That was when I started to really look at the meaning of love. What does it mean to love someone? What does it mean to love the Lord with all my heart, soul, and mind, as the Scripture commands? I began my search with the description of love given in First Corinthians 13. This Scripture told me the behaviors I would have if I loved. I would be patient; I would be kind; I would not envy; I would not boast; I would not be rude; I would not be self-seeking; I would not be easily angered; I would not keep records of wrongdoings; I would not delight in evil; I would always protect; I would always trust; I would always hope; and I would always persevere.

Still I wondered, What exactly is love? I needed to know what love is! When I looked in the dictionary, I found that *love* is defined as "a feeling of deep affection or passion; strong affection arising out of closeness and kinship." *Passion* is defined as "a strong feeling of love, anger, hope, desire, joy, fear, or grief." Often these forces compel our behavior. *Affection* was defined as "settled good will, love or zealous attachment." Therefore, *love* is a strong passionate feeling with a compelling force that gives a settled zealous attachment.

I told the Lord, "Father God, I want to have a love for You that is this strong." I want to have a strong passionate feeling with a compelling force that gives me a settled zealous attachment that will stand up to all competing emotions. I want to be able to say to any competing emotion that comes into my life:

"I need God more than I need anything else."

Needing God more than anything else could apply to so many different things in a person's life. Think about the alcoholic or the drug addict. He needs to be able to say to any thoughts of addictions that would come before God in his life, "No! I want God more than I want you."

Think about the person involved in an ungodly relationship. He needs to be able to say to that ungodly desire, "No! I want God more than I want you."

Think about the person obsessed with money. He needs to be able to say to that lust for money, "No! I want God more than I want money."

I want you to be able to say to any competing emotion that would compel you to put your faith and love for the Father on the back burner, "No! I want God more than I want you."

During this time when I was searching for answers, I realized that much of my love in the past had been rooted in selfishness and control. I found myself crying out to the Lord in repentance and crying out for the Lord to teach me His ways, to teach me how to love.

Grappling With the Issue of Love

While I was trying to grapple with this issue of love, the Father started revealing to me that I did not understand how much He loved me. I found myself saying, "Lord, how do I understand Your love?" In my mind I started reviewing Scriptures on the Father's love. I first thought of John 3:16: "For God so loved the world, that He gave His only begotten Son,

that whosoever believeth in Him should not perish,
but have everlasting life."

I remembered that Jesus said in John 17:3 (NIV),
"Now this is eternal life: that they may know You, the
only true God, and Jesus Christ, whom You have sent."

What He started showing me was that once I tapped
into the knowledge and the understanding of His love
for me, I would struggle less to obey Him. So I started
asking the Father, "What is it I do not understand about
You? Why have I served You for 25 years and yet I still do
not truly understand how much You love me? What has
blocked this fullness of information?"

The Lord quickly brought to my mind the parable
of the sower in Matthew 13:1-23. Jesus explained to the
disciples the meaning of the parable:

> *When anyone hears the message about the kingdom
> and does not understand it, the evil one comes and
> snatches away what was sown in his heart. This is the
> seed sown along the path. The one who received the seed
> that fell on rocky places is the man who hears the word
> and at once receives it with joy. But since he has no
> root, he lasts only a short time. When trouble or perse-
> cution comes because of the word, he quickly falls away.
> The one who received the seed that fell among the
> thorns is the man who hears the word, but the worries
> of this life and the deceitfulness of wealth choke it,
> making it unfruitful. But the one who received the
> seed that fell on good soil is the man who hears the
> word and understands it. He produces a crop, yield-
> ing a hundred, sixty or thirty times what was sown*
> (Matthew 13:19-23 NIV).

From that Scripture I saw that understanding is interrupted by the evil one snatching the Word away; understanding is interrupted by troubles and persecution; and understanding is interrupted by the deceitfulness of wealth. Also, I felt that the Lord revealed that I still had doubts about His great love for His children. I asked the Lord, "Why? Why do I still have doubts?"

Then I felt Him say, "You have listened to the enemy many times when you should have been reciting Scripture to him. There has been a shortage of messages on My love. Many people have heard many sermons on judgment and not enough on My love and My abundant blessings."

I began to understand that this is not about me; it is about the great love the Father has for me. Until that time I felt that much of my Christian walk was dependent on what I did. For example, if I obeyed all God's commandments, He would love me; if I read the Bible daily, He would love me; if I went to church every time the doors were open, He would love me; if I prayed regularly and fasted, He would love me. My entire relationship with God was, in my eyes, dependent upon what *I* did. All of a sudden I saw that I was not the perfect person I had always thought myself to be. How was God going to deal with me? This is what the Father taught me.

To Help Me Choose Right,
The Father Taught Me a Different Way to Pray

The Father started showing me different prayers to pray. These prayers required the Lord to do something for me. My whole emphasis in prayer shifted.

I have strayed like a lost sheep. Seek Your servant, for I have not forgotten Your commands (Psalm 119:176 NIV).

First, the Lord showed me that I should ask Him to seek me out. The Psalmist knew that he had sinned. Apparently he felt weak, since he asked God to seek him.

Seek Me, Lord

Ask God to seek you out with great persistence. Ask Him not to allow you to hide from Him. Ask Him to find you even if you are hidden behind several walls.

Once the Father has found you, you need to pray another kind of prayer. King David shows us how to pray like this.

The Bible says that David was a man after God's own heart:

...the Lord has sought out a man after His own heart and appointed him leader of His people.... (1 Samuel 13:14 NIV).

God had chosen him and blessed him. But David found out that his desires were not always God's desires for him:

Then David sent messengers to get her [Bathsheba]. *She came to him, and he slept with her...* (2 Samuel 11:4 NIV).

If you are not familiar with this account of David, please take time to read the Book of Second Samuel. After God had made him king, David sinned greatly. Psalm 51, a beautiful prayer, records David's repentance after he had committed adultery with Bathsheba (see 2 Sam. 11). In this prayer David asks, "Create in me a pure heart, O God, and renew a steadfast spirit within me" (Ps. 51:10 NIV).

David asked God to create in him a pure heart. It is interesting to me that David did not ask God to *restore* in him a pure heart. *Create* is a word that means something entirely different from *restore*. *Create* means to bring something into existence, something that has not previously been there.

Create a Pure Heart in Me, Lord

David apparently felt that he had never had a pure heart in that area, or he would have asked God to restore his pure heart. *Restore* means to renew or rebuild. David was saying, "Father, create in me a heart that is pure and wants to obey You." David was saying, "Father, bring that pure heart into existence for me."

David knew he could not pray enough or fast enough or go to church enough to bring this pure heart into existence. He knew that the Father had to do this for him.

Make Me Hear You, Lord

David, a man after God's own heart, knowingly and willingly sinned against the Father. David loved God, but his heart was not right. In Psalm 143:8, David told the Lord, "Cause me to hear Thy lovingkindness...."

In other words, "Lord, make me do Your will. Lord, I need You to help me hear You and to give me the strength necessary to respond to You." If you read the entire Book of Psalms, you will see that David often cried out to the Lord, asking the Lord to deliver him. Sometimes David wanted deliverance from outside enemies; sometimes he himself was the enemy.

When your heart is not right, your own heart is your worst enemy. Then you need to cry out to the Father, asking Him to rearrange your desires. Perhaps your behavior is the result of an unmet need and you need God to show you your need and heal you. Or you may be engaging in behavior that is sinful and destructive, and you need to ask God to help you stop. This cannot happen until you ask God to reveal why you are involved in this particular behavior. For example, you might ask Him, What need is this behavior filling in my life? Can this need be met in a more healthy, less sinful way?

Let's use the example of an alcoholic. He may be drinking because of a chemical imbalance. Instead of praying through and getting direction from the Father, he continues drinking. If he had prayed for some direction, God could have healed him instantly.

The same is true for you. Ask God to show you why you persist in a particular behavior. You may be led to a person who operates in the gift of healing so you can be healed. Or you may be led to go see a mental health professional who will prescribe a medication for a short while or even longer or who will help you process your past. Whatever your need, God will direct you when you seek His counsel.

Many people are against seeking professional help for depression, anxiety disorders, and addiction. Although they continue to be easily irritated and easily frustrated, they still refuse to seek professional help. I realize that not all professional help is good help. However, you need to be in prayer and believe that God is a big enough God to lead you to the proper place. Wouldn't you consider going to the doctor to get medicine if you had a sore throat and suspected you had strep throat? Look in Matthew 9:12 (NIV), "On hearing this, Jesus said, 'It is not the healthy who need a doctor, but the sick.' "

There is a conflict between faith and medicine that I wish did not exist. I believe that God heals. Sometimes the healing is instantaneous, and sometimes you have to go dip in the Jordan seven times. In Second Kings 5:10, Elisha told Naaman to go wash in the Jordan River seven times and he would be healed. Naaman did not like those instructions. He wanted Elisha to speak the word and heal him.

Many of us want God to speak the word and heal us. When God uses another means of healing besides the instantaneous, we get upset. It is as if we have no faith if we allow ourselves to take medicine. I believe that if we take everything to the Father with prayer and supplication, we can have 100 percent assurance that our God will lead us and direct us. He may heal us instantly or He may lead us to get some salve. The decision is His. Our part is to pray, ask, and obey.

Realize Your Need to Be Taught God's Ways

Another thing you need to keep in mind is the word *teach*. For some reason, we Christians feel that we are supposed to automatically know what to do when we get saved. It is the same way in marriage. We get married and automatically assume that we should know all there is to know about marriage.

What I see is, we do *not* automatically know what to do. For instance, take the Book of Psalms in the Bible. In Psalm 119, the Psalmist asked God ten times to teach him His ways. You would think that someone who could write like that would know the ways of God. However, that is a trick of the devil. The devil tries to convince us that we know more than we really do know.

We do not automatically know how to love. We do not automatically know how to crucify the flesh. We need encouragement and instruction.

In Exodus 33:13 (NIV), Moses said to God:

If You are pleased with me, teach me Your ways so I may know You and continue to find favor with You....

By this point in Moses' life, he had seen many, many miracles. He had seen the plagues that God had sent on the Egyptian people. He had seen the Red Sea part. He had seen Father God send manna and quail for the children of Israel to eat daily. He had seen a rock miraculously start pouring out water. Moses had seen and experienced many spiritual things. He believed God. He feared God. Yet he still needed God to teach him because he understood that he had much to learn about God's ways.

Doing the right thing does not just automatically happen. We need to be taught how to resist temptations. We need to be taught how to love. We need to ask

God to create a pure heart inside of us. Just because we have seen the Lord do great things does not mean that we will never again need to be taught. Living for God and with God is a daily process. There is much the Father wants to teach us.

The Bible says that those who overcome will enter the Kingdom of Heaven (see Rev. 2–3). *Overcome* means to conquer. Who must you conquer? What must you conquer? You must conquer your desire to do the wrong thing. Struggling is okay. Giving up is not.

Let's review before we go on to the next chapter:

1. Realize that righteous people before you have struggled to do the right thing.

2. Realize that God accepts you because of what Jesus did on the cross and not because of what you have done to deserve His love and attention.

3. Ask God to seek you out (see Ps. 119:176).

4. Ask God to create in you a pure heart (see Ps. 51:10).

5. Realize that you need to be taught (see Ps. 119; Ex. 33:13).

6. Realize that you may enjoy sin for a season. That does not mean it is right.

7. Realize that you may be your own worst enemy.

8. Realize that change is hard. Get your mind ready for a battle with yourself.

9. You may feel overwhelmed at times when you struggle. That's okay. Jesus was overwhelmed

with sorrow when He chose to do the right
thing (see Mt. 26:38).

10. Ask God to give you courage (see Josh. 1).

11. Have absolute assurance that you will feel better
    and be victorious as you abide with the Father.

* * *

*Holy Father, I come to You today on behalf of each and every
person who may be reading this chapter. Father, cause them
to understand that You really care about their struggle, that
You really care that things have been less than fulfilling in
their lives. I believe, Father, that they have sought comfort in
many ways, hoping to feel better. They have developed some
habits and thought structures that they must break with Your
help.*

*Father, some feel helpless; others feel powerless. They need
You to help rescue them from themselves. Father, bless them
today with revelation knowledge that You are the God who
heals them, that they can count on You. Please seek them out
and rescue them from themselves. Father, breathe on all who
read this book. Breathe on their needs and fill them with
Your presence. Grant them insight to understand Your great
love for them. Let them now feel a significant difference in
their hearts and in their being.*

*O Father, we are like the disciples; if we can't come to You,
where do we go? You are our only hope.*

*Let Your healing power fall on these readers. Holy Father,
give them the ability to fight and win. Let them be tenacious Christians—Christians who do not run from a fight
with themselves when they know that Your way is right.*

Holy Father, empower them to resist the devil and all his luring temptations.

Father, pour out Your unconditional love on all who read this book. May their love for You increase. May their passion for You increase. Father, may they experience who You are and be convinced of Your ability to meet their desires. In Jesus' name. Amen.

Chapter 10

The Lord Will Fight for You!

Then I said to you, "Do not be terrified; do not be afraid of them. The Lord your God, who is going before you, will fight for you, as He did for you in Egypt, before your very eyes, and in the desert. There you saw how the Lord your God carried you, as a father carries his son, all the way you went until you reached this place" (Deuteronomy 1:29-31 NIV).

Knowing this is crucial for someone who has tried to change a behavior or a situation and has been unsuccessful. Changing is an absolute fight! In your fight to change, the temptation not to can be great at times. There are going to be times in your life when the only thing that keeps you emotionally afloat is the fact that God will fight for His children. You must have and use the information from this chapter in order to be sustained during those times.

Several times in my life I have felt that if God did not intervene and help me fight, I was going to lose the battle. It is very important for you to recognize and understand this feeling. Sometimes we feel so helpless in our ability to change. Sometimes the circumstances are so overwhelming that only a miracle will save the situation. Many times people who come to me for counseling or who attend one of my seminars need to be encouraged to believe that God is who He says He is. It is essential for anyone in any type of recovery to understand that God will fight for them no matter how hard it is to change.

I have been saved and serving the Lord for 25 years. Until the last few years, I never realized how powerful the Father God is. I have experienced several situations that I know would not have been handled successfully unless Father God had done something to cause them to work out. These situations involved my having a change of heart or a change of desire.

I Needed God to Fight for My Will!

I needed God to create in me a heart so pure toward Him that I would lose my desire for anything else that was competing for my emotions. I knew the Scripture said that God could change a king's heart.

The king's heart is in the hand of the Lord; He directs it like a watercourse wherever He pleases (Proverbs 21:1 NIV).

My reasoning was, if God has the ability to change a king's heart, then certainly He can change my heart. When you allow the Father to change your heart, you are going on a journey from bondage to your own selfish desires to freedom so you can allow the Father to teach you about His desires.

This is not an easy process. We like ourselves. We like our thoughts and our desires. When you submit your thoughts and desires to the Father, you feel like you do not know who you are. You may feel blank. When you begin letting God take control of your desires and emotions, God starts building a new you.

This cannot happen until you truly give God the opportunity to show you a new way. God can then start helping you develop the person you have always wanted to be. This is exciting. However, it is also threatening. You want to yield to the Father, but you do not want to give up who you are. You will have to have confidence in the Father to allow Him to make these necessary changes. You must believe that God wants, more than you do, for you to develop into the person you have always wanted to be and into the person He knows you can be. As you yield to the Father, He will help you understand your heart.

Over the years there have been significant Scriptures that have helped me relinquish my will into the Father's hand. I share these Scriptures because this is how the Lord taught me this most valuable lesson.

God Fought for the Israelites and I Knew He Would Fight for Me

The Book of Exodus tells the history of Moses leading the children of Israel out of Egyptian bondage. This book has become one of my favorites because I can see myself on that journey. The children of Israel were making a physical journey from bondage in Egypt to freedom in the promised land. We are making an emotional and spiritual journey from all the bondages of negative thoughts and actions to the freedom of making positive choices and enjoying a personal relationship with the Father God, His precious Son Jesus, and our loved ones.

There were several difficult things about that journey the Israelites made. God told Moses that He would deliver them from Egypt. However, Moses had to believe that God was going to be there to back him up. He had to work to get prepared for the journey. The livestock had to be prepared. The material possessions of the Israelites had to be packed and prepared for a journey. Moses had to be prepared to mentally fight himself. Moses also had to fight the other people's unbelief.

Moses could have said, "God, why didn't You fight for us 400 years ago? Why did You let this happen to Your chosen people? If You loved us, Lord, why has the happened to us? Lord, why did You allow us to stay in bondage 400 years? Why are You so concerned now?"

Some of you may be feeling what I just described. "Why now, Lord?" Just because you are feeling that way does not mean God is not dealing with you now and that He does not love you. It means you are confused about where God was during your difficult times and confused about how to connect with and understand God.

Many times you cannot comprehend that God will fight for you. This is not natural for you. Your natural feeling is to believe that you must do everything on your own. You understand that if you do not work, you do not eat. You do not understand this:

Come, all you who are thirsty, come to the waters; and you who have no money, come, buy and eat! Come, buy wine and milk without money and without cost. Why spend money on what is not bread, and your labor on what does not satisfy? Listen, listen to Me, and eat what is good, and your soul will delight in the richest of fare (Isaiah 55:1-2 NIV).

This is a real Scripture of faith. If you have never been around people of real faith, this Scripture and other Scriptures in this chapter about God fighting for you, may be foreign to you. The concept of God actually physically doing something for you is hard for you to digest. You may not have a script in your mind that reminds you that God is an active, alive God.

Let me share something with you about our minds. When we are faced with any kind of task, we first review our minds to see if we have any information that will help us complete the task or solve the problem. That is what some call a *script*. To me, a script is a set of information.

Now, if you are faced with a situation that seems impossible, you may feel that you have to give up because you have no information stored away that will help you solve the problem. What I want to do today is write a new script for you to store in your mind. That script will be information regarding the Holy Father God fighting for you. This is a characteristic that is vital to your successful walk with the Father.

Scriptural Evidence That God Will Fight for His People

In the Book of Exodus, Moses had an enormous task ahead of him. At first he did not want to obey the

Lord. Remember all the excuses he gave the Father before he finally submitted? Moses realized the kind of difficulty that lay ahead of him.

God is going to fight for His people throughout the journey. I want to share with you some Scriptures the Lord has written into my heart. It has helped me to remember what the Lord did for people who lived long before me. When the Israelites were about to come up to the Red Sea Moses spoke in faith. Look at Exodus 14:13-14 (NIV):

Moses answered the people, "Do not be afraid. Stand firm and you will see the deliverance the Lord will bring you today. The Egyptians you see today you will never see again. The Lord will fight for you; you need only to be still."

In verse 22 the Israelites did go through the Red Sea on dry land. In that same chapter in verse 25, the Egyptians realized that God the Father was fighting for the Israelites:

He [God] *made the wheels of their chariots come off so that they had difficulty driving. And the Egyptians said, "Let's get away from the Israelites! The Lord is fighting for them against Egypt"* (Ex. 14:25 NIV).

I am giving you these accounts for a purpose. I want you to see, as I saw, that the Scriptures supports the evidence that God will fight for His people—and if you are a Christian, you are one of His people. In the Book of Deuteronomy, Moses made speech after speech to the children of Israel just before they crossed the Jordan into the promised land. Moses reminded them that the Lord had fought for them throughout their journey.

Then I said to you, "Do not be terrified; do not be afraid of them. The Lord your God, who is going before you, will fight for you, as He did for you in Egypt, before your very eyes, and in the desert. There you saw how the Lord your God carried you, as a father carries his son, all the way you went until you reached this place" (Deuteronomy 1:29-31 NIV).

Some of you reading this may feel that you need to be carried for a while. At times the load of life and all its responsibilities feels overwhelming. This is the time you need to be encouraged and reminded of how powerful God is. He has led you by His Holy Spirit to this book today. It is not an accident you are reading right now. Please be encouraged. Your understanding is going to increase! Your joy is going to increase! You must continue searching for the Father and His Son and the precious Holy Spirit.

Let's keep looking at Scripture. In Deuteronomy 3:22 (NIV), Moses reminded the people:

Do not be afraid of them; the Lord your God Himself will fight for you.

In Deuteronomy 20:4 (NIV), Moses said:

For the Lord your God is the one who goes with you to fight for you against your enemies to give you victory.

King Jehoshaphat in Second Chronicles 20 was one of the better kings of Judah. In the following account he was surrounded by his enemies, the Ammonites and the Moabites. He realized he was facing a hopeless situation unless the Lord intervened. When the Spirit of the Lord came on one of the Levites, Jahaziel, he told the king:

> *He said: "Listen, King Jehoshaphat and all who live in Judah and Jerusalem! This is what the Lord says to you: 'Do not be afraid or discouraged because of this vast army. For the battle is not yours, but God's. Tomorrow march down against them. They will be climbing up by the Pass of Ziz, and you will find them at the end of the gorge in the Desert of Jeruel. You will not have to fight this battle. Take your positions; stand firm and see the deliverance the Lord will give you, O Judah and Jerusalem. Do not be afraid; do not be discouraged. Go out to face them tomorrow, and the Lord will be with you' "* (2 Chronicles 20:15-17 NIV).

It was a great day for me when I started seeing all these Scriptures. Now I had scriptural evidence that the Father would fight for His children. In the past, I have personally cried, "Father, I am so weak in this particular situation. If You do not fight for me, I do not see how I can change." When I remembered these Scriptures, I had hope.

Don't Get Discouraged if You Feel Powerless to Change

There is one more Scripture I want to give you that has been meaningful to me. In Second Chronicles 14, King Asa was facing his own set of enemies:

> *Then Asa called to the Lord his God and said, "Lord, there is no one like You to help the powerless against the mighty. Help us, O Lord our God, for we rely on You, and in Your name we have come against this*

vast army. O Lord, You are our God; do not let man prevail against You" (2 Chronicles 14:11 NIV).

You may feel at times that you are powerless against the mighty—"the mighty" being your desire for things in your life that are separating you from God's best for you. King Asa said, "In Your name we have come against this vast army."

You may have a vast army arrayed against you right now, an army quite different from that of King Asa. Your army may be an army of thoughts telling you that you must have drugs, alcohol, food, unhealthy relationships, money, etc. You could be an alcoholic, a drug addict, a gambler, an overeater, or a person involved in an ungodly relationship, and you feel that the army of thoughts pulling you toward this behavior is more than you can handle. You feel that you desperately need the Lord to fight for you.

I have felt that way at times. That is when I cried out to the Father, "Make me do Your will, O Lord!" That is when I said, "Cause me to desire Your ways!"

You must face your desires. You must cry out to the Father and say, "These desires are not good, and I realize that they are not good." You must say to God, "Do whatever You have to do to correct my heart."

God has proven to me that He will fight for me. I had to get to a point where I was open to the Lord fighting for me. I was desperate. I felt like no one but the Lord God could help. I had to be able to see the possibility of the Lord actually fighting for me.

It is awesome when you are able to grab hold of that concept, when you start seeing God actually moving on your behalf. This has been an essential revelation from God to me. I hope you will also be able to grasp this truth deep in your being.

Throughout these Scriptures, the main themes have been courage and faith—faith to believe the Lord will fight for you, and courage to remain firm in your belief. Discouragement is our enemy. Satan tries to discourage us and make us lose faith in the Lord.

We must fight our minds as Moses had to fight his mind. That is why there are so many Scriptures telling us to be strong and courageous. Our minds control our level of discouragement. When we have filled our minds with God's Word, we will be in better shape spiritually when the attacks come from the enemy. Satan comes to rob us of our confidence (see Jn. 10:10)—our confidence in the Father's ability to rescue us in our time of need.

The Bible says in Exodus 15:3 (NIV),

The Lord is a warrior, the Lord is His name.

In Psalm 24:8 (NIV) the Bible says:

Who is this King of glory? The Lord strong and mighty, the Lord mighty in battle.

God told Abraham in Genesis 15:1 (NIV):

...Do not be afraid, Abram. I am your shield, your very great reward.

So from all these Scriptures we have an image of our God as a warrior—a warrior familiar with battle. Nevertheless, even if we try to understand God, and we see from the Bible, which is a history of God, that it is His will to do battle for us, there may still be times when we will have to battle with ourselves to believe that it will happen. We have to exercise a certain amount of faith that God will fight for *us*. In the moment we choose to believe God, we relinquish our control of the situation. We acknowledge that God is in control and we are not. This moment can be very difficult because most of us do not like the idea of relinquishing control.

As you wait for the Lord to move in your life, you must have tenacity. *Tenacity* means not being easily pulled away. You must be firmly fixed on your position that the Lord will fight for you.

Guard Against Fear and Weariness

There are two things you need to guard against when trying to be tenacious. These two things are fear and weariness. If you give into them they will make you give up. Fear is the opposite of courage. It will make you give up quickly. Weariness, on the other hand, makes you give up a little at a time. Both are tactics that satan uses to defeat you.

Fighting and Overcoming

In the second and third chapters of Revelation there are several Scriptures that show us the importance of overcoming. *Overcoming* suggests winning after a hard struggle. Think about this for a few moments. Revelations 3:5 (NIV) says:

He who overcomes will, like them, be dressed in white. I will never blot out his name from the book of life, but will acknowledge his name before My Father and His angels.

Our struggle is generally with ourselves. We struggle at times to believe. We struggle to give up control and to ask God to have His complete way in our lives.

You Must Learn to Fight God's Way

The Bible is quite specific in giving instructions on how to fight the evil one. One of the main areas of instruction is Ephesians 6:

> *Finally, my brethren, be strong in the Lord, and in the power of His might. Put on the whole armour of God, that ye may be able to stand against the wiles of the devil. For we wrestle not against flesh and blood, but against principalities, against powers, against the rulers of the darkness of this world, against spiritual wickedness in high places. Wherefore take unto you the whole armour of God, that ye may be able to withstand in the evil day, and having done all, to stand. Stand therefore, having your loins girt about with truth, and having on the breastplate of righteousness; and your feet shod with the preparation of the gospel of peace; above all, taking the shield of faith, wherewith ye shall be able to quench all the fiery darts of the wicked. And take the helmet of salvation, and the sword of the Spirit, which is the word of God* (Ephesians 6:10-17).

Everything Is Under the Feet of Jesus

The Scriptures say that God gave Jesus authority over everything and put everything under His feet. Every power of the devil is under the feet of Jesus. Ephesians 1:22 (NIV) says, "And God placed all things under His [Jesus'] feet and appointed Him to be head over everything for the church." Hebrews 2:8a (NIV) says, "And put everything under His feet...."

The Scripture says that when we accept Jesus as our Lord and Savior, we are co-heirs with Jesus.

Now if we are children [children of the Father], *then we are heirs—heirs of God and co-heirs with Christ, if indeed we share in His sufferings in order that we may also share in His glory* (Romans 8:17 NIV).

Another book could be written on the authority the believer has once he accepts Jesus and grabs hold of all the promises in the Bible. Jesus' death gave us straight access to the Father. We have the Holy Spirit to guide us and Jesus' finished work on the cross to equip us. In First Corinthians Paul teaches us about the gifts that are available to us as believers. We can overcome the devil.

Pray

Jesus prayed for His followers in John 17:

I pray not that Thou shouldest take them out of the world, but that Thou shouldest keep them from the evil (John 17:15).

Jesus prayed that the disciples would be kept from evil. We need to pray this for one another just as Jesus prayed for the disciples.

Understand Who Has All the Authority

If there is a void in this understanding, you will not be able to come against the devil in your life. When you start studying the Bible, you will see that much of your time will be spent fighting the devil. This is what we call *spiritual warfare*.

This too could be the subject of another book. For the sake of this one, I want you to remember that the devil would like to rob, steal, and destroy your mind, your heart, and your life.

God is all-knowing. God is all-powerful. God is all-present. God knows everything. God is more powerful than any being or person in this earth and the universe. God is omnipresent. God is not limited by time or space. But, most of all, that same powerful God wants to have a relationship with you. The Bible says in Revelation 4:11:

Thou art worthy, O Lord, to receive glory and honour and power: for Thou hast created all things, and for Thy pleasure they are and were created.

We were created for God's good pleasure. He created us out of His own will. We are not an accident. God wants to enjoy us. God wants us to enjoy Him.

You must understand that God is more powerful than satan and all his demons. This authority that God has, He chose to give to Jesus. According to the Bible we are joint-heirs with Christ; therefore, being a Christian is a powerful person to be.

Jesus Was Manifest to Destroy the Works of the Devil

The Bible says that Jesus had a purpose in coming: "For this purpose the Son of God was manifested, that He might destroy the works of the devil" (1 Jn. 3:8b).

We are joint-heirs with Jesus. We are to continue the work He did. You and I, through the power of the Lord Jesus, are to destroy the works of the devil.

Jesus Wants to Help You Overcome

In Hebrews 4:15-16 (TLB) Paul tells us that Jesus is also our High Priest:

This High Priest of ours understands our weaknesses, since He had the same temptations we do, though He never once gave way to them and sinned. So let us come boldly to the very throne of God and stay there to receive His mercy and to find grace to help us in our times of need.

Paul says for us to come boldly to the throne of God and ask for help. The Living Bible says to stay there until you receive mercy and help. *Mercy* is undeserved favor. Sometimes we need help to see, help to understand, and help to fight.

God does not want His authority to be something you resent or regard as controlling. He wants His authority to be something you trust and value. Through Jesus God wants to give you His authority. God knew that you were going to need authority to fight the enemy. His ammunition is available to you. You must trust the Father.

Let's review:

1. Moses could have asked God why He didn't rescue the Israelites earlier, but he did not.

2. Think about the times in your life that you needed an intervention from God. What made you give up?

3. Review the fight Scriptures. Write them on a piece of paper. Carry them in your purse or pocket. Read them to yourself every day for the next 60 days. This will help you battle your negative thoughts and actions.

Then Asa called to the Lord his God and said, "Lord, there is no one like You to help the powerless against the mighty. Help us, O Lord our God, for we rely on You, and in Your name we have come against this vast army. O Lord, You are our God; do not let man prevail against You" (2 Chronicles 14:11 NIV).

The Lord will fight for you; you need only to be still (Exodus 14:14 NIV)

He made the wheels of their chariots come off so that they had difficulty driving. And the Egyptians said, "Let's get away from the Israelites! The Lord is fighting for them against Egypt" (Exodus 14:25 NIV).

Do not be afraid of them; the Lord your God Himself will fight for you (Deuteronomy 3:22 NIV).

For the Lord your God is the one who goes with you to fight for you against your enemies to give you victory (Deuteronomy 20:4 NIV).

Wherever you hear the sound of the trumpet, join us there. Our God will fight for us! (Nehemiah 4:20 NIV)

He said: "Listen, King Jehoshaphat and all who live in Judah and Jerusalem! This is what the Lord says to you: 'Do not be afraid or discouraged because of this vast army. For the battle is not yours, but God's. Tomorrow march down against them. They will be climbing up by the Pass of Ziz, and you will find them at the end of the gorge in the Desert of Jeruel. You will not have to fight this battle. Take up your positions; stand firm and see the deliverance the Lord will give you, O Judah and

*Jerusalem. Do not be afraid; do not be discouraged.
Go out to face them tomorrow, and the Lord will be
with you' "* (2 Chronicles 20:15-17 NIV).

4. Realize that you will have to fight yourself until
   you are firmly rooted and established in the Lord.

5. Pray Ephesians 3:16-21 (NIV) aloud. Put your
   name in the prayer. Ask God to do those things
   for you that Paul wanted done for the Ephesians.

6. Remember that you will go through a process
   of training your mind the right way to think—
   the faith way!

7. Outline for yourself the army of thoughts and
   actions that you need to have captured by the
   Father. Ask the Lord to fight for you in those
   areas in which you are weak.

8. Recognize fear and weariness for what they are:
   tactics of the devil. Fear quenches faith quickly,
   and weariness is a slow death to faith.

* * *

*Holy Father, mighty God, make us, Your children, see the reality
of Your power. Father, help us grasp Your love that surpasses
knowledge. Holy Father, help us be rooted and established in
Your love. Father, we need Your strength to take all this in. We
ask You today to reveal to us more about Your nature and
ways, and especially about Your desire to fight for us. Father,
You told Abraham that You would be his shield. Father, be
our shield. Shield us from doubt and disbelief. Father, we are
like the man in Mark 9:24—we do believe, but we need You to
help us overcome our unbelief. When we are struggling with
problems such as fear, weariness, and destructive behaviors,*

Father, let us know You will fight for us. Father, do great things before our eyes. Let us see You move on our behalf. In Jesus' name. Amen.

Chapter 11

Balancing Understanding and Faith

But it is the spirit in a man, the breath of the Almighty, that gives him understanding (Job 32:8 NIV).

Consider what I say; and the Lord give thee understanding in all things (2 Timothy 2:7).

You may be feeling, "Why has this happened to me? What did I do to deserve this pain?" What if the answer is that you did not do anything to deserve it?

How Much Should You Try to Understand?

Many times we resist grappling with ourselves because we do not feel that we have the right to question God. We may feel that things are too complicated to understand.

Have you ever asked, "How much understanding should one have in regard to negative things that happen in life?" I have asked that question. When a person pursues faith in God, how much should he understand? How much do we need to know about ourselves? How important is knowledge? How do we get that balance between knowledge and faith?

The Bible has helped answer these questions for me. In Colossians 2:2-3 (NIV) it says,

> *My purpose is that they may be encouraged in heart and united in love, so that they may have the full riches of complete understanding, in order that they may know the mystery of God, namely, Christ, in whom are hidden all the treasures of wisdom and knowledge.*

Paul says that all the treasures of wisdom and knowledge are hidden in the Father and the Son. Knowledge is referred to as a treasure.

Also, we see this in Psalm 51:6 (NIV): "Surely You desire truth in the inner parts; You teach me wisdom in the inmost place." David said that the Lord desired truth in the "inner parts." There are many scriptural references to the word *truth* in the Bible.

In John's Gospel, there are several references to the truth: "...the *truth* will set you free" (Jn. 8:32 NIV); "...the Spirit of *truth*, is come, He will guide you into all *truth*" (Jn. 16:13a).

Paul spoke of the "belt of truth" in Ephesians 6:14: "Stand firm then, with the belt of *truth* buckled around your waist...."

The Scriptures place a great emphasis on truth. The word *truth* means the true or actual facts of a case. The word *true* means being in accordance with the actual state of things. When we are looking at ourselves, we need to know the actual state of things in our being.

Many times we do not understand or know the actual state of our being. I believe that is why Paul instructs us in Ephesians to put on the belt of truth. We have a great promise in the Scriptures that the Holy Spirit will guide us into all truth. In John 16:13 (NIV), the Bible states, "But when He, the Spirit of truth, comes, He will guide you into all truth."

Therefore, I think we can safely say that we need faith and we need truth. Truth involves knowing the actual state of yourself. You cannot know the truth until you have understanding.

God wants you to understand the meaning of your feelings and behaviors. The word *understanding* means to perceive the meaning of a thing. Thus to have understanding about yourself is to perceive the meaning of what is happening within you and why you act as you do.

I believe that the Father wants to give us understanding. Job 32:8 (NIV) says, "But it is the spirit in a man, the breath of the Almighty, that gives him understanding." Paul told Timothy in Second Timothy 2:7, "Consider what I say; and the Lord give thee understanding in all things."

Paul wanted Timothy to have understanding in all things. All things! I believe that means understanding all areas of our lives. I think we can safely say that God desires for us to have understanding and to walk in faith.

Don't Give Up Looking for Answers

The conclusion I finally came to was that it is okay to not have all my questions answered. I was able to let go of some of my search when I saw that different people in the Bible had searched and come up with very similar conclusions.

There is value in learning as much as we can. I had to try to gain some understanding of why God allows evil. Still, we do not have to understand all God's ways. Nevertheless, it is far better and more fulfilling to have as much understanding as we can, even if we agree that we do not have the total answer.

Many before us have tried to answer this question. I want us to consider the experiences of several people in the Bible when they sought God trying to answer this same question.

Jeremiah and Job are two men who questioned God. It seems that both were saying, "If You are an all-powerful God and have all authority, why are You allowing these things to happen?" Both of these men received answers that only made me keep searching.

Jeremiah

Jeremiah 12 and 20 recount Jeremiah's experience when he asked God, "Why do the wicked prosper?"

You are always righteous, O Lord, when I bring a case before You. Yet I would speak with You about Your justice: Why does the way of the wicked prosper? Why do all the faithless live at ease? You have planted them, and they have taken root; they grow and bear fruit. You are always on their lips but far from their hearts. Yet You know me, O Lord; You see me and test my thoughts about You. Drag them off like sheep to be butchered! Set them apart for the day of slaughter! How long will the land lie parched and the grass in every field be withered? Because those who live in it are wicked, the animals and birds have perished. Moreover, the people are saying, "He will not see what happens to us" (Jeremiah 12:1-4 NIV).

Jeremiah was asking a good question. God answers Jeremiah in verse 5 of chapter 12:

If you have raced with men on foot and they have worn you out, how can you compete with horses? If you stumble in safe country, how will you manage in the thickets by the Jordan? (Jeremiah 12:5 NIV)

God seems to be saying to Jeremiah that his hard times had not yet begun. In essence, the Lord was saying, "Jeremiah, you must trust Me in all this."

Job

In the Book of Job we have another account of a man questioning God. Job was suffering greatly and he wanted understanding. The Bible relates that Job was a righteous man who served the Lord. In the first chapter God draws satan's attention to Job, His faithful servant. Satan questions Job's fidelity, saying that the only reason Job served God was because God had blessed him with great protection and blessings. God then gave satan permission to test Job.

Job was distressed because of all the loss and suffering that God was allowing him to experience at the hands of the devil, so Job started asking why. If you read the Book of Job, you will soon see that it does not give us a great deal more information than the Book of Jeremiah gives.

Brace yourself like a man; I will question you, and you shall answer Me. Where were you when I laid the earth's foundation? Tell Me, if you understand. Who marked off its dimensions? Surely you know! Who stretched a measuring line across it? On what were its footings set, or who laid its cornerstone—while the morning stars sang together and all the angels shouted for joy? (Job 38:3-7 NIV)

God was saying, "There is a lot you do not understand, Job."

So, we see two great men of God who questioned God's sovereignty and did not get the answers they wanted. However, we see that God did not punish either man for questioning Him. God's response let them know that there were things they did not understand.

God Wants You to Understand How Much He Loves You

Understanding brings something to our relationship with God that mere obedience does not. If we obey the Lord for the sake of obeying, that is good. There are plenty of times when we do things simply because we are obeying the Lord. If, however, we talk with the Lord and reason with Him, and the time we spend with Him brings understanding to a certain situation, then our relationship with Him is enriched and enhanced.

I want your relationship with the Lord to be enriched and enhanced as you read, because I want this book to bring understanding to your heart, soul, and mind. I want you to understand what authority all believers have because Jesus died for us.

*   *   *

*Father, bring understanding to my heart and mind today.
Father, You did not cause any bad thing to happen to me.
Help me to understand that You did not leave me defenseless
and helpless to deal with the enemy. Father, You have always
had a salvation plan for me, if I would accept it. Help me desire to know You so intimately that I will have great understanding of the spiritual resources you have provided for me.
Father, I do understand that You love me and that You are
offering me salvation, healing, deliverance, and guidance.
In Jesus' name. Amen.*

Chapter 12

Surrendering to the Sovereignty of God

The mighty deep cried out, announcing its surrender to the Lord (Habakkuk 3:10b TLB).

It has taken me quite a while to understand the value of Father God's authority. As long as you do not really understand that, you will be a wounded, crippled Christian. Your ability to fight the different things life throws at you will be measured by your understanding of God's authority over everything. You can serve the Lord wounded and you can serve the Lord crippled; but your effectiveness will be limited. I believe that God is calling loudly to His children that it is time to get things right. God wants a relationship with you. He wants you to be part of His family. He wants you to understand how much He loves you. The Father has work for you to do for Him. Satan wants to keep you bound. Jesus wants to set you free.

Is God Sovereign?

The word *sovereign* means having supreme power or authority. In God's case there is no power or authority that is stronger or greater. Do you believe that God has ultimate authority? If you do, that means everything and everybody is subordinate to God. Some may be comforted by that; others may be angered.

My desire to write this chapter is not to take a scholarly approach. Many exhaustive books have been written on God's sovereignty and on the origin of evil. My desire is to strike at the heart of the matter as honestly as I can to encourage us toward a greater love for God and His precious Son, Jesus.

There are special problems associated with abused people and their relationship to authority; I have tried to help you understand that connection. The only way I could personally tackle answering the question raised in the title of this book was to settle in my own mind whether or not I truly believe that God is completely sovereign. A belief in the sovereignty of God has to be experienced. No one can take this subject to a laboratory and physically examine the answer. Out of my personal life experiences I am convinced that God is all-powerful.

I realize that I do not have to understand God's ways in order to worship Him, love Him, or trust Him. I do not know why He did not destroy satan and his angels at the time they rebelled. Wouldn't that have prevented evil forever? Nor do I know why God put the tree of the knowledge of good and evil in the Garden, but He did. Likewise, I have had to cry out to the Father because I do not know why He does not abolish evil now.

Perhaps you wonder why God let something bad happen to you. I do not believe God caused or commissioned it; nevertheless, because I believe that God is sovereign, I have to say He did permit everything that has happened.

We have to decide that it's okay if we don't have all the answers. We have to respect God's ways even when we might not understand all His purposes. Then, in spite of our unanswered questions, we have to get on with our lives.

This was not extremely difficult for me to do. I think the reason I have had little trouble accepting this is because I know the Father; I know He loves us. I know He cares about our pain and wants to hear from us about our suffering.

One thing that has been consoling to me is that God has been consistent in what He has required for reconciliation to Him. In the Old Testament God required reconciliation by the shedding of blood. In the New Testament God's plan for reconciliation with Him continued to involve the shedding of blood.

The blood that was to be shed once and for all was the blood of Jesus Christ our Savior. Jesus was the ultimate sacrifice; there could be no greater or better. Jesus shed His blood for you and for me. His death gave us access to the Father.

I say all this to explain how valuable Jesus is to us and to review what Christianity is about. You may be feeling in your heart that you are not sure how you feel about God's plan of salvation. God designed the plan without any input from us. You may not believe that. That does not make it untrue, but it means you are having difficulty accepting God's plan.

If you are in rebellion, you may have trouble accepting anybody's plan. If you are emotionally injured and you have not received healing, you may have trouble trusting anyone. We have no problems with authority when we trust the person in control. We might not understand everything, but we have respect for God. We must believe that God is looking out for our best interests when we trust Him.

Why Does God Allow Evil?

I believe that evil originated from satan. I believe satan fell from Heaven as the Bible describes in Isaiah 14:12-14:

How art thou fallen from heaven, O Lucifer, son of the morning! how art thou cut down to the ground, which didst weaken the nations! For thou hast said in thine heart, I will ascend into heaven, I will exalt my throne above the stars of God: I will sit also upon the mount of the congregation, in the sides of the north: I will ascend above the heights of the clouds; I will be the most High.

At the time satan was cast from Heaven, he was named Lucifer. Look at Revelation 12:9:

And the great dragon was cast out, that old serpent, called the Devil, and Satan, which deceiveth the whole world: he was cast out into the earth, and his angels were cast out with him.

Satan took his angels with him, and I believe that he and his angels are working against you and me at all times. In Job 1:7 (NIV) the Bible says, "The Lord said to Satan, 'Where have you come from?' Satan answered the Lord, 'From roaming through the earth and going back and forth in it.' "

Take that Scripture and compare it with John 10:10:

The thief [satan] *cometh not, but for to steal, and to kill, and to destroy: I am come that they might have life, and that they might have it more abundantly.*

Jesus was telling the people that satan came to rob from them, steal from them, and destroy them. Satan wants to rob you of peace and happiness.

Peter, in his writings, stated, "Be sober, be vigilant; because your adversary the devil, as a roaring lion, walketh about, seeking whom he may devour" (1 Pet. 5:8). He wants to destroy your family, your marriage, and your children.

In the last part of John 10:10, Jesus said that He came so that you might have life and have it more abundantly. Satan is the evil one. Since God is sovereign, we have to come to the agreement that if something exists, He allows it to exist. We are now looking at our questions. Could God have allowed evil so we could have a clear choice between good and evil?

I Believe God Wants Us to Choose Him

God does not want to make us serve Him. God wants genuine love from us, not forced love or obligated love. You may not like the idea that God gave us a clear choice. You may not like it that God has allowed evil to exist. I believe that God gives us free will to choose Him or reject Him. God permits free moral agents to choose good or bad. This choice can't be limited in any way, or we would be persuaded one way or the other.

I Do Not Believe God Causes Bad Things To Happen to Us

The Bible is a book of salvation. God is trying to save us. Save us from what? God wants to save us from so many destructive things. He wants us to trust Him and enter into a personal relationship with Him and He promises to teach us how to overcome the devil. God's plan for us involves a close personal relationship.

Can You Love God Knowing He Allows Evil?

As I tried to answer this question, I started thinking of people in the Bible who had been abused. I wanted to look at these accounts and see how these people handled their situations. I was particularly interested in their attitudes toward their abusers and toward the Father for allowing the abuse.

Joseph

Joseph was Jacob's eleventh son. He was Rachel's first son. Until his birth Rachel had been barren. When Joseph was a young boy, his mother died bearing his brother, Benjamin. Joseph was probably no more than ten years old when his mother died. Perhaps Jacob coddled Joseph and treated him as the favored son because he had lost his mother and the other sons had their mothers. In any case, Joseph's brothers hated him and sold him as a slave to a band of Ishmaelites when Joseph was 17.

In Egypt Joseph was bought by Potiphar, an Egyptian officer and captain of the guard. In time Joseph demonstrated such diligence that he was put in charge of Potiphar's entire household and affairs. One day Potiphar's wife tried to seduce Joseph, but he refused her advances. To get her revenge, she told her husband that Joseph had tried to violate her. Joseph ended up in jail.

Joseph soon gained the trust of the prison warden and was put over the other prisoners. Pharaoh's cupbearer and head baker were put into prison. Joseph's interpretation of the cupbearer's dream came true. The cupbearer was released as Joseph had predicted. Later, Pharaoh needed a dream interpreted and the cupbearer remembered Joseph. Joseph interpreted the dream and Pharaoh was so impressed that he decided to give Joseph power in his kingdom.

Under Joseph's direction, Egypt prepared for famine. When the famine struck Canaan, Jacob's other sons went to Egypt to find food. In Egypt they found their brother alive. (See Genesis 37–50.)

Let's review the losses Joseph had suffered:

1. He lost his mother.

2. He lost the love of his brothers.

3. He lost his family at age 17.

4. He lost all security except God.

5. He lost his job at Potiphar's house.

6. He lost his freedom due to imprisonment.

It is interesting to see how Joseph handled every loss. He never gave up. He worked hard no matter where he was, no matter what the situation was. Most importantly, through all his hard times he was able to release his bitterness toward his brothers (see Gen. 45:7). Joseph explained to his brothers that he held no grudge against them for what had happened to him:

> *And God sent me before you to preserve you a posterity in the earth, and to save your lives by a great deliverance. So now it was not you that sent me hither, but God: and He hath made me a father to Pharaoh, and lord of all his house, and a ruler throughout all the land of Egypt* (Genesis 45:7-8).

Joseph never forgot God through all his suffering. I believe that Joseph learned a great deal about himself during this hard time.

I gave you a summary of Joseph's life. What I did not emphasize is that he probably spent many lonely nights wondering why this happened to him. Yet, he did not stay in that mind-set. He chose to move on and stay faithful to God. His final conclusion was that God was working all things out for good (see Rom. 8:28).

In God's time things *will* work for good. Look at the way Joseph comforted his brothers who had abused him:

> *But as for you, ye thought evil against me; but God meant it unto good, to bring to pass, as it is this day, to save much people alive. Now therefore fear ye not: I will nourish you, and your little ones. And he comforted them, and spake kindly unto them* (Genesis 50:20-21).

Joseph learned an attitude that we should all strive to attain. That is to care for our abusers. That is a hard attitude to have if you are still bitter because of harm done to you. Joseph was able to love his brothers, as well as God, in spite of the abuse he had suffered. God blessed his attitude. Joseph is a perfect example of loving God even though He allowed evil to touch his life.

Jesus

The most significant abuse of all is the crucifixion of our Lord and Savior Jesus Christ. Jesus had done no wrong. He did not deserve the treatment He received.

If I Do Not Believe God Knew About the Abuse, How Can I Believe God Can Heal and Comfort Now?

As we have seen, the answer to the question, "Where was God when I cried?" is that God was there. He was with me all the time. The same is true for you. If I did not believe God knew about the abuse, how could I believe He could heal you and comfort you now? God knows your pain. He knows your hurts. That is why He is reaching out to you now. He alone knows the depth of your betrayal. He cares about you. If you are to access God's love, you must choose the Father and accept His Son, Jesus. You must also believe that God has good in store for you.

Habakkuk

There is one more person in the Old Testament whom I feel sheds a great deal of light on this subject about God and the existence of evil. Habakkuk is a very short book, having only three chapters. It consists of a conversation between God and Habakkuk, in which Habakkuk asks why a sovereign God allows evil to go unpunished.

Habakkuk lived between the fall of the northern and southern kingdoms. He was a prophet to the southern kingdom of Judah. The northern kingdom, Israel, had fallen to Assyria a few years earlier. During the time Habakkuk lived, the political situation looked very desperate. There was inner turmoil in Judah. The legal system was weakening, and there were oppressive measures against the poor. The threat of an invasion from Babylon only added to the problems Judah was experiencing. Habakkuk opens the book by questioning God.

> *O Lord, how long must I call for help before You will listen? I shout to You in vain; there is no answer. "Help! Murder!" I cry, but no one comes to save. Must I forever see this sin and sadness all around me? Wherever I look there is oppression and bribery and men who love to argue and to fight. The law is not enforced and there is no justice given in the courts, for the wicked far outnumber the righteous, and bribes and trickery prevail* (Habakkuk 1:2-4 TLB).

Habakkuk longed for an answer from God. He was perplexed because God was allowing all the evil to go on around him. He wondered why the evil was going unpunished. Thus his concern was similar to Jeremiah's complaint. Both asked why the wicked prospered. In essence, Habakkuk was saying, "Why does a sovereign God allow this to go on?"

This is what we are asking in this book. The Lord told Habakkuk that the fierce Babylonians were going to be used by God to bring judgment on the Judeans.

Look at the nations and watch—and be utterly amazed. For I am going to do something in your days that you would not believe, even if you were told. I am raising up the Babylonians, that ruthless and impetuous people, who sweep across the whole earth to seize dwelling places not their own. They are a feared and dreaded people; they are a law to themselves and promote their own honor. Their horses are swifter than leopards, fiercer than wolves at dusk. Their cavalry gallops headlong; their horsemen come from afar. They fly like a vulture swooping to devour; they all come bent on violence. Their hordes advance like a desert wind and gather prisoners like sand. They deride kings and scoff at rulers. They laugh at all fortified cities; they build earthen ramps and capture them. Then they sweep past like the wind and go on—guilty men, whose own strength is their god (Habakkuk 1:5-11 NIV)

Habakkuk did not like God's response.

O Lord, are You not from everlasting? My God, my Holy One, we will not die. O Lord, You have appointed them to execute judgment; O Rock, You have ordained them to punish. Your eyes are too pure to look on evil; You cannot tolerate wrong. Why then do You tolerate the treacherous? Why are You silent while the wicked swallow up those more righteous than themselves? You have made men like fish in the sea, like sea creatures that have no ruler. The wicked foe pulls all of them up with hooks, he catches them in his net, he gathers them up in his dragnet; and so he rejoices and is glad. Therefore he sacrifices to his net and burns incense to his dragnet, for by his net he lives in luxury and enjoys the choicest food. Is he to keep on emptying his net, destroying nations without mercy? (Habakkuk 1:12-17 NIV)

The Lord responded to Habakkuk and told him to write down what was going to happen.

Then the Lord replied: "Write down the revelation and make it plain on tablets so that a herald may run with it. ... See, he is puffed up; his desires are not upright—but the righteous will live by his faith—indeed, wine betrays him; he is arrogant and never at rest. Because he is as greedy as the grave and like death is never satisfied, he gathers to himself all the nations and takes captive all the peoples.

"Will not all of them taunt him with ridicule and scorn, saying, 'Woe to him who piles up stolen goods and makes himself wealthy by extortion! How long must this go on?' Will not your debtors suddenly arise? Will they not wake up and make you tremble? Then you will become their victim. Because you have plundered many nations, the peoples who are left will plunder you. For you have shed man's blood; you have destroyed lands and cities and everyone in them.

"Woe to him who builds his realm by unjust gain to set his nest on high, to escape the clutches of ruin! You have plotted the ruin of many peoples, shaming your own house and forfeiting your life. The stones of the

wall will cry out, and the beams of the woodwork will echo it.

"Woe to him who builds a city with bloodshed and establishes a town by crime! Has not the Lord Almighty determined that the people's labor is only fuel for the fire, that the nations exhaust themselves for nothing? For the earth will be filled with the knowledge of the glory of the Lord, as the waters cover the sea.

"Woe to him who gives drink to his neighbors, pouring it from the wineskin till they are drunk, so that he can gaze on their naked bodies. You will be filled with shame instead of glory. Now it is your turn! Drink and be exposed! The cup from the Lord's right hand is coming around to you, and disgrace will cover your glory. The violence you have done to Lebanon will overwhelm you, and your destruction of animals will terrify you. For you have shed man's blood; you have destroyed lands and cities and everyone in them.

"Of what value is an idol, since a man has carved it? Or an image that teaches lies? For he who makes it trusts in his own creation; he makes idols that cannot speak. Woe to him who says to wood, 'Come to life!' Or to lifeless stone, 'Wake up!' Can it give guidance? It is covered with gold and silver; there is no breath in it. But the Lord is in His holy temple; let all the earth be silent before Him" (Habakkuk 2:2,4-20 NIV).

Habakkuk could not understand why God was going to use a cruel army like the Babylonians to deal with the Judeans. The Lord explains in chapter 2 the crimes the Babylonians had committed and He promises that He will deal with them also.

I interpret the last verse in chapter 2 as God saying, "I am judging from My holy temple, and people need to be silent." God knew that we could not totally understand His judgments and His timing; therefore we need to be silent. However, this is a response that is somewhat perplexing. God gave Jeremiah and Job a somewhat perplexing response to their questions also. In Habakkuk 2:4 (TLB), the Lord says, "The righteous man trusts in Me, and lives!"

The Righteous Trust Me

Before God tells Habakkuk what He has against the Babylonians, He tells Habakkuk that the righteous *trust in Him.* This statement seems almost to slip into the conversation. However, it is the whole essence of God's message to Habakkuk. Romans 1:17 parallels exactly with this Scripture: "For therein is the righteousness of God revealed from faith to faith: as it is written, The just shall live by faith."

This Scripture gives us the impression that God's righteousness is revealed only through faith. The questions we have been discussing have been questioning God's righteousness, but God says through Paul in this verse in Romans that His righteousness is revealed from faith to faith.

I believe "from faith to faith" means that as our faith grows, we understand more of Christ's and the Father's righteousness. No one can really answer these questions for another. Each individual must grapple independently with this issue of God allowing evil. You must have some level of faith in order to have peace about God and evil. There has to be some level of surrender on your part, just as Habakkuk said in 3:10b (TLB): "The mighty deep cried out, announcing its surrender to the Lord."

This Scripture was referring to God's influence on the earth as God moved across the land. As God moves across your being, I pray that you will yield to Him deep within and surrender totally to His authority. There has to be a time of surrender. In this process of questioning God, you must surrender to God's judgment; you must surrender to God's plan.

Surrendering Is Different From Accepting

Accepting means to receive with approval. Accepting generally needs some level of understanding. *Surrender* means yielding to the power of another. Surrendering requires faith. We need understanding, but we also need faith. We may understand, but we may not like what we understand. That is where each person must decide deep within whether or not he is going to surrender to God.

Habakkuk announced his surrendering to the Lord in chapter 3. After Habakkuk hears what God's plans are, he no longer desires an answer.

Something spiritual happened to Habakkuk's heart in between the second and third chapters. Habakkuk closed the book in an entirely different state of mind. He closed with a prayer asking God to revive His people and exalting God's greatness. Finally Habakkuk made a declaration of his own consecration to the Father.

Though the fig tree does not bud and there are no grapes on the vines, though the olive crop fails and the fields produce no food, though there are no sheep in the pen and no cattle in the stalls, yet I will rejoice in the Lord, I will be joyful in God my Savior. The Sovereign Lord is my strength; He makes my feet like the feet of a deer, He enables me to go on the heights (Habakkuk 3:17-19a NIV).

Habakkuk was saying that regardless of the circumstances, he would rejoice in the Lord. *Habakkuk changed once he encountered the Father.* He encountered the Father because he started asking the Father questions. I want to invite you to ask God questions. When you ask Him and you do not understand what He says to you, ask Him again.

When you ask God questions, you open communication so the Holy Spirit can teach you. If you do not ask, you do not learn. If Habakkuk had not questioned God, he would not have received the information that he did.

After God included Habakkuk in what was going to happen, Habakkuk said that in spite of what he saw, he would rejoice in the Lord. Habakkuk went from confusion to absolute faith. Habakkuk knew that in God's own time He would deal with all the injustice he was witnessing.

The Bible clearly states that vengeance is the Lord's. Romans 12:19b says: "Vengeance is Mine; I will repay, saith the Lord."

The Power of a Touch From the Father

Habakkuk gained understanding from the Father. There is something so awesome and powerful about God, that when His presence touches our lives, we are quieted. We are not quieted in that we can never question again, but in that we know the Almighty can be trusted. His judgment on why He has allowed evil can be trusted and even defended. His presence is full of absolute assurance that we can trust His decision. We receive assurance that we can confide our care to Him!

Embrace Me, Lord

The word *Habakkuk* comes from a Hebrew root meaning to "embrace." Habakkuk was embraced by God and strengthened by God through his conversation with the Almighty God. Habakkuk did not get the answer he was looking for. However, his response in chapter 3 indicates that he apparently received something even greater. The Almighty Sovereign God shared with Habakkuk His future plans.

Once Habakkuk was embraced by the Father, he learned to rest in God's judgments. *Embrace* means to clasp in the arms physically. Mentally it means to include as a part of the whole. I believe that God wants to share with you an understanding about yourself and about Him.

When understanding comes, you feel included, as though you are part of the plans of the Almighty God. Then your attitudes change, your fears are released, and your faith becomes alive and active. When understanding comes and you realize why you have been acting or thinking a certain way, you become more confident. When confidence begins, then you can change.

Once you trust God and His direction, you start feeling more secure. Once you feel welcomed, cherished, and loved by the Father, your ability to trust the Father dramatically increases.

You may be asking, "How does the Almighty God embrace me?" He embraces you by letting you experience His presence. He embraces you by giving you understanding about yourself that makes you feel God's personal interest in your life. When this happens, you feel included in the Almighty's design for you. I believe that is what the Lord wants to do for each person who is reading this book. God wants you to experience His presence, His power, and His love for you.

Finding Your Place

After you are over the hurdle of being at peace with God and the existence of evil, you must find your place in Him. Many realize that God is a big enough God to have designed things the way He did. What they need help in is finding their place in Him, or finding their position in Him.

Where do we fit in? What is our job? Many do believe that God is all-loving. They just do not know how to have a personal, fulfilling relationship with Him. That is a greater issue in their lives.

How do we break through and be a part of God's life? Many believe that it is possible because they know people who have broken through. Still they are not sure how they can break through to have their own personal fulfilling relationship with God. Saying, "Just have faith" does not seem to work for them. Neither does just saying, "I believe." They need a breakthrough. They need a clear understanding of what is blocking their spiritual connection with God.

What happened to you in the past is not as important as what you do about what has happened to you. Do you allow the hurtful events in your life to destroy you or do you allow an Almighty God to help you make sense out of things? Do you allow the walls you have built out of necessity destroy your ability to love the Lord and the people closest to you? Do you believe that God is reaching out to you today to reveal to you a higher plan for your life—a plan you did not realize existed? Can you grasp the idea that just because you suffered greatly at some point in your life, your life is not over?

The Real You

The real you may still be hidden. The real you may be looking for ways to take down the walls you use to protect yourself. The real you wants to love the Father and to embrace and love your family. The real you yearns for verbal expression to flow from your mouth, letting God and others know that you really care.

You must be willing to tell satan that he no longer has power over your mind. You are the Father's child, the holy Father's child. You are no longer alone. You are no longer abandoned! You are no longer rejected! *You* have been accepted and included by the Holy Father God! You have been included in the family of families. God's plan for your life has not been aborted. Remember these two Scriptures: "The Lord will perfect that which concerneth me..." (Ps. 138:8), and "He hath made every thing beautiful in His time..." (Eccles. 3:11).

Now, my friend, take this information and know that you are on the road to a fabulous journey with the Father.

We Have Hope!

We have hope today because we have a God who has designed a plan that will enable us to overcome. We have hope today because we have a God who is constantly sending out invitations to us, saying, "Let Me help you with your life." We have hope today because this God sent His Son, Jesus, to be our Savior. We have hope today because everything is under the feet of Jesus. We have hope today because Jesus came that we might have life and have it to the fullest (see Jn 10:10b). We have hope today because the Holy Spirit was sent to counsel us, guide us, comfort us, and teach us. We have hope today because the Father promised He would never leave us or forsake us. We have hope today because Jesus came to heal the brokenhearted. We have hope today because every sin we have ever committed or will commit is covered by the precious blood of Jesus. We have hope today because Father God included a plan for us to join Christ in the work He started.

We are not alone. We have the Holy Father and His precious Son, Jesus, as well as the Holy Spirit to walk through life with us. There is no one or no being that is more powerful or more knowledgeable than God.

You are in a position of safety. You are in a position of great security. You do not have to face tomorrow alone. God Himself has left you numerous Scriptures indicating that faith is the essence of Christianity. One of my favorites is Hebrews 11:6:

> *But without faith it is impossible to please Him: for he that cometh to God must believe that He is, and that He is a rewarder of them that diligently seek Him.*

God Wants to Include You

You must feel included before you can rest in that faith. Furthermore, feeling included does not mean you never have another question. *God wants questions to come to your mind because it drives you to Him.* When you question God, it shows that you still care. If you didn't care at all, you would not even bother to ask Him any questions. He wants to be able to furnish you with peace when no one else can. You need to constantly be turning to the Father for answers.

God wants to be valued. He wants you to appreciate His ways. God is not withholding things from you. He is trying to teach you to come to Him when you are in need because many times, He will be the only one who can help. He wants you to know that He will never leave you or forsake you (see Heb. 13:5).

People will hurt you. They are human like you and me. But you can totally trust the Father. God requires you to trust Him. If you have faith, all the promises of God are available to you. Satan very much wants to block this message because he does not want you to realize the full life you would have by totally following Father God. God promises you many things in His Word. You must realize that satan is your enemy; it is not your past that is your enemy. God will heal your past. The questions now are, "Will you trust the Father?" and "Can you serve a God who gave His Son for you to be saved?"

* * *

Father God, exalt our understanding of You. Father, in the powerful name of Jesus I ask You to communicate Your love to us. Father, I know Your love is filling. Your love is satisfying. Father, let us experience Your filling, satisfying love today. Father, You communicated something to Habakkuk that was life-changing. Father, reveal to us as You revealed to Habakkuk information that will encourage us. Father, Habakkuk was so moved by Your conversation with him that he was willing to serve You and rejoice in You no matter what his past or present circumstances were. Father, Habakkuk was going to serve You even if his crops failed and his barn was empty. Father, let us be like the deer Habakkuk spoke of that swiftly scaled the mountain. Father, help us scale the mountains of abuse, abandonments, rejection, and neglect in our lives and help us feel safe and secure as we continue on our journey with You. In Jesus' name. Amen.

Points of Faith to Remember

1. Ask God to give you the gift of faith that Paul spoke about in First Corinthians 12:1-9: "Now concerning spiritual gifts, brethren, I would not have you ignorant....For to one is given by the Spirit the word of wisdom; to another the word of knowledge by the same Spirit; to another faith by the same Spirit....." You need to know that faith is a gift and that faith can be gained by knowing God's Word. In Romans 10:17 the Bible says, "So then faith cometh by hearing, and hearing by the word of God." Faith comes by hearing God's Word. Read the Word aloud, especially on the days you are down.

2. Read about the life of Joseph. Genesis 37–50 gives the account of Joseph's life. The reason that story will be faith-lifting to you is because

Joseph was abandoned and rejected by his brothers. He suffered from a dysfunctional family. Look at how Joseph felt about his brothers when they finally realized who he was.

3. Read about Esther in the Book of Esther. Esther had no living mother or father; she was reared by a cousin. Esther was fearful to go into the king without being summoned by him. Esther turned to the Lord in prayer and fasting to help her work through her fear. Consider fasting. Begin today to study everything you can on fasting. (Beginners need to consider a partial fast.)

4. Remember a Scripture that is very important when you want revenge for what has been done to you. "...Vengeance is Mine, I will repay, saith the Lord" (Rom. 12:19).

5. If you do not feel healed, please go back and read this book again. Sometimes you have been healed but you feel like you are not healed. This may be the time to seek some godly counsel to help you discern the truth.

6. If you are having trouble obeying the Lord, re-read Chapters 6, 8, and 9. Remember Jesus' prayers in the Garden of Gethsemane.

7. If you have read the book, truly sought the Lord, and still feel like you are struggling, please consider seeking further counseling, which may need to be from a professional or pastoral counselor.

8. Keep asking questions! Because Habakkuk, Job, Jeremiah, and others asked questions, they all

became closer to God. Their questions enhanced their relationship with the Father.

9. Ask yourself, "Have I totally surrendered to God and the Lord Jesus Christ?" Then ask yourself, "Have I announced that surrender in my day-to-day life?"

Have a great journey with the Father!

Appendix A

This book would not be complete without some final words on forgiveness and discipline. I have mentioned these two areas briefly. Just because I did not emphasize these two elements of a Christian's life, though, does not mean that they are not important. Rather, it means this book is primarily on healing. Once you do experience the healing power of the Lord Jesus Christ, you then need to ask the Father to help you stay connected to the Holy Spirit. Two fruits of the Holy Spirit are love and self-control (see Gal. 5:22-23). As you continue to follow the Lord's guidance, your self-control and love will naturally grow. When you start producing love as a fruit of the Spirit, your ability to forgive will become more evident. Forgiveness may be harder for you than self-control, or vice versa. Either way, they are two musts in your Christian life.

In this book I shared with you my prayer for some of my clients, that God would give them a gift of forgiveness. When you start asking the Lord to help you forgive, you will need to be able to forgive the person who has hurt you. You will also need to forgive yourself and God. It is easy to understand the need for forgiveness toward the person or persons who hurt you; however, you will also have to deal with yourself. You probably have said things and done things that you wished you had not said or done. You must forgive yourself and let this book be a benchmark in your life, a place to start over. Repent, ask God to forgive you, and be determined to move on.

You must forgive God. You may not realize that you are offended at God, but chances are that you are offended at Him. You have been thinking that if He is all-powerful, why couldn't He have let things turn out differently? You must repent and surrender those feelings to the Lord. You will never bear much fruit for the Father until you deal with these areas of forgiveness. When you are totally in love with the Father God and the Lord Jesus Christ, the discipline, or self-control, does not take as much effort. Love for the Father and Jesus will lead you to the Bible and to prayer. My prayer for you, the readers of this book, is for you to fall completely in love with our Lord and Savior Jesus Christ, and our Father God.

Appendix B

I would like to invite anyone who is unsure about his salvation to please read this prayer and seal his relationship with the Lord today.

Heavenly Father, I believe Jesus Christ is Your only begotten Son. I ask Jesus to come into my heart and life today. I believe that Jesus came and lived on this earth, died on the cross for my sins, and rose from the dead on the third day. I believe that He is at the right hand of the Father making intercession for the believers right now. I ask You, Father, to forgive me of my sins. Father, I accept Jesus as my Lord and Savior. I thank You for sending Him and I thank Jesus for coming and dying for my sins so I could have life and have it abundantly. Father, strengthen me through Your Word. Teach me about Your Holy Spirit. Help me never to quench the Holy Spirit. Father, let the Holy Spirit's gifts and the fruits be active in my life. Father, I love You today. I desire to please You. Teach me Your ways. In Jesus' name. Amen.

Appendix C

Chapter Verses

Chapter 1

For we have not an high priest which cannot be touched with the feeling of our infirmities; but was in all points tempted like as we are, yet without sin. Let us therefore come boldly unto the throne of grace, that we may obtain mercy, and find grace to help in time of need (Hebrews 4:15-16).

Chapter 2

He heals the brokenhearted and binds up their wounds (Psalm 147:3 NIV).

Chapter 3

If an enemy were insulting me, I could endure it; if a foe were raising himself against me, I could hide from him. But it is you, a man like myself, my companion, my close friend, with whom I once enjoyed sweet fellowship as we walked with the throng at the house of God (Psalm 55:12-14 NIV).

Chapter 4

Surely You desire truth in the inner parts; You teach me wisdom in the inmost place (Psalm 51:6 NIV).

Chapter 5

Heal me, O Lord, and I will be healed (Jeremiah 17:14a NIV).

"But I will restore you to health and heal your wounds," declares the Lord (Jeremiah 30:17a NIV).

Chapter 6

Get rid of all bitterness, rage and anger... (Ephesians 4:31 NIV).

For man's anger does not bring about the righteous life that God desires (James 1:20 NIV).

Chapter 7

There is a way which seemeth right unto a man, but the end thereof are the ways of death (Proverbs 14:12).

Chapter 8

Being confident of this very thing, that He which hath begun a good work in you will perform it until the day of Jesus Christ (Philippians 1:6).

Chapter 9

...nevertheless not as I will, but as Thou wilt (Matthew 26:39).

Chapter 10

Then I said to you, "Do not be terrified; do not be afraid of them. The Lord your God, who is going before you, will fight for you, as He did for you in Egypt, before your very eyes, and in the desert. There you saw how the Lord your God carried you, as a father carries his son, all the way you went until you reached this place" (Deuteronomy 1:29-31 NIV).

Chapter 11

But it is the spirit in a man, the breath of the Almighty, that gives him understanding (Job 32:8 NIV).

Consider what I say, and the Lord give thee understanding in all things (2 Timothy 2:7).

Chapter 12

The mighty deep cried out, announcing its surrender to the Lord (Habakkuk 3:10b TLB).

Other
Destiny Image titles
you will enjoy reading

Other
Destiny Image titles
you will enjoy reading

LADY IN WAITING
by Debby Jones and Jackie Kendall.
This is not just another book for singles! With humor, honesty, and biblical truths, the authors help all women—married or single—to passionately pursue a personal relationship with Jesus, and to seek His perspective on their life and future.
ISBN 1-56043-848-7 $9.99p

LADY IN WAITING
Devotional Journal and Study Guide
by Debby Jones and Jackie Kendall.
You can keep the principles taught in *Lady in Waiting* in your heart by learning to apply them with this devotional journal and study guide. These questions, quotes, thoughts, and teachings will help you to become the woman of God that He designed you to be. You also can record your spiritual growth in a specially designed journal section. Don't miss this opportunity to become God's "Lady in Waiting"!
ISBN 1-56043-298-5 $7.99p

HOW TO AVOID A BOZO—*NEW VIDEO*
Help for Finding God's Best in a Mate
by Jackie Kendall.
Do you want to find God's best—Mr. Right? Learn the differences between a man worth waiting for and a Bozo. Don't let your lover be a loser!
1 video ISBN 0-7684-0070-8 Retail $14.99

Available at your local Christian bookstore.
Internet: http://www.reapernet.com

Prices subject to change without notice.   2:45